KB067275

Doing Ethics
in the Narcissistic Age

| Doing Ethics in the Narcissistic Age |

1st printing July 3, 2020 ⓒ 2020 by Yong Sup Song

Dong-Yeon Press
    Address: 2nd FL. #163-3 Worldcup-Ro, Mapo-Ku, Seoul, Korea
    Tel: +82-2-335-2630 Fax: +82-2-335-2640
    e-mail: h-4321@daum.net / yh4321@gmail.com
    Publication registration number: 1-1383(1992. 6. 12)

ISBN 978-89-6447-591-1 93190

이 도서의 국립중앙도서관 출판예정도서목록(CIP)은 서지정보유통지원시스템 홈페이지
(http://seoji.nl.go.kr)와 국가자료종합목록 구축시스템(http://kolis-net.nl.go.kr)
에서 이용하실 수 있습니다. (CIP제어번호 : CIP2020027310)

Doing Ethics
in the Narcissistic Age

| Yong Sup Song |

동연

| Preface |

We live in a narcissistic age today. The social problems and events we encounter on the news are increasingly involved in people who experience excessive narcissistic anger and exhibitionism. They are often pathological narcissists who have not experienced mature love and proper care since childhood from their parents or have experienced physical and emotional abuse. It is easy to see that when they try to satisfy their narcissistic needs without empathizing with the pain of others, more serious and accidental problems will emerge in our society.

However, one of the reasons why children experience the absence of parents, as Heinz Kohut once concerned, may be the problem of industrialization, which forced their parents to work without enough time and conditions to take care of their children. The neoliberal social structure of our time that creates a vicious cycle of infinite competition further exacerbates the problems of parental absence and of the lack of care and love at home.

Therefore, the cause of the social problems that an individual commits is not only the families in which the individual grew up as a child, but also the unempathic and unjust social structure that produced those families. Therefore, the cause of the sociopathological events that we experience today is not only a personal problem of the members of our society, but also the social structural problems, which are both psychological and ethical.

In this book, *Doing Ethics in the Narcissistic Age*, I have dealt with these personal, social, ethical and psychological issues through three topics: "Doing Ethics, Toward Sustainable Justice, and Heinz Kohut and Narcissism." The previous two ethical papers introduce existing ethical theories about social problems, and attempt to construct my own ethical methodologies based on the theories. The third paper is a part of my doctoral dissertation. This paper introduces

Kohut's narcissism and argues for its applicability to the fields of ethics. I hope that this book will provide an opportunity for us to live an ethical life in the Narcissist era.

| contents |

preface _ 5

First   **Doing Ethics: A Hermeneutic Spiral**   11

field   1. Introduction _ 13

           2. Hermeneutic Spiral _ 15

           3. Application of A Hermeneutic Spiral _ 37

           4. Conclusion _ 59

           Bibliography _ 62

Second   **Toward Sustainable Justice**   65

field   1. Introduction _ 67

           2. Starting Points _ 69

           3. Problems of Theories of Justice _ 76

           4. Elements for fan Alternative Concept of
              Justice _ 91

5. Descriptions of Justice _ 105

6. Conclusion: Toward Sustainable Justice _ 118

Bibliography _ 121

Third   **Heinz Kohut and Narcissism**   123

field   1. Developments in Understanding Narcissism

          _ 125

          2. Kohut's Psychology of the Self: Aspects of

          Narcissism _ 133

          3. Conclusion _ 160

          Bibliography _ 162

I

Doing Ethics:
A Hermeneutic Spiral

1. Introduction

This essay studies the meaning and function of ideology in doing ethics. People may think and act differently according to their knowledge and understanding of the world. Because their understanding of the world may provide either justification of a status quo, or, the dynamics of social change, it is important to learn how we can develop methodology that is helpful for the ethical life of a person as moral agent and subject. In order to do so, we need to understand the meaning and functions of ideology in relation with our ethical decision making process and subsequent action.

This essay argues that our construction of a methodology should critically reflect a historically situated self and that of others. In doing so, we expand our previous ideological limitations to overlapping common ideas, norms, and values. In developing my argument, this essay introduces my own methodology of a hermeneutic spiral. In describing my methodology, I believe that a hermeneutic spiral is valid because our perspective and understanding of the Bible and the world should be changing continuously and should seek to be expanded toward a more common consensus, especially, when reflecting on the poor and marginalized. I apply it to the issue of the National Security Law in South Korea, and suggest some elements of overlapping common references in our doing ethics as a moral agent and subject.

Some themes that I emphasize in the process of the development of the arguments as such: Peace, justice, life, relationality-responsibility, concrete reality, praxis for liberation, and conscientization. Our construction of a new methodology that reflects these themes would help us aware that we are moral agents and subjects and would encourage us to live an ethical life in the process of the development of the hermeneutic spiral.

2. Hermeneutic Spiral

In this chapter, I attempt to construct my methodology of doing ethics. I will elaborate this idea in dialogue with Manheim, Pieris, and Segundo's explanation of ideology. My ideas are, however, mostly indebted to the ideas of Manheim and Segundo.

I have identified my methodology of doing ethics as a *hermeneutic spiral*. Influenced by Segundo, I argue that our interpretation of the Bible and the world should be dynamic, that is, in continuum, based on the influence of continuous change in the individual and in societal realities. In addition, Manheim's understanding of the total conception of ideology helps one to formulate an idea that an interpretation should be self-critical and be expanded upon the basis of how we have previously been grounded. As a result, there may be contact points found with those to be in continuum with the process of interpretive expansions.

In terms of a hermeneutic spiral, the fundamental basis of the interpretation of the Bible and the world is grounded in our own concrete situation. These hermeneutic lenses should start from our own subjective experiences and thoughts of present realities in our lives, and are tested by our critical reflection. The hermeneutic lenses can be expanded by sharing such experiences and ideas with those of others. In the process of the expansion, like a spiral, we continuously come back to our present realities that change continuously day by day. However, these processes of circulation in understanding realities and sharing experiences gradually broaden our interpretative worldview. These continuous circulations of critical hermeneutic reflections resemble the shape of spiral that expands from the ground towards broader areas.

My concept of a hermeneutic spiral resembles Segundo's ideas of the hermeneutic circle. That is, Segundo defines the hermeneutic circle as "the continuing change in our interpretation of the Bible which is dictated by the continuing changes in our present-day reality, both individual and societal."[1] Segundo continues that the questions out of the present reality should be "rich enough, general enough, and basic enough to force us to change our customary conceptions of life, death, knowledge, society, politics, and the world in general."[2] In addition, he argues that our new interpretation should be profound enough to change traditional interpretation of the Bible.[3]

My argument is consistent with Segundo's concept of the hermeneutic circle in that it suggests our interpretive perspectives to be continuously changing in the reflection of the

---

1) Juan Luis Segundo, *The Liberation of Theology* (Maryknoll: Orbis Books, 1982), 8.

2) *Ibid.*

3) *Ibid.*, 9.

changes of the realities of the world. However, my concept of a hermeneutic spiral is more dynamic and is describing the movement of our interpretive perspectives toward overlapping common ones. Thus, I am suggesting that our methodology should be broadened and can be shared with and be appealing to more people who can identify with it.

I suggest four steps in the process of a hermeneutic spiral. I will use following racist comments on Koreans as an example of the exercise of hermeneutic spiral at the end of each hermeneutic step.

> *Example:*
>
> *"You, Koreans, are sneaky people. You do not look at my eyes when you speak to me."*

I call the first step as *hermeneutic negation.* This is a necessary and courageous process for us to open possibilities of changes in our unexamined ideologies. In this step, we should be, at least *temporarily,* able to negate ideologies, norms, and values that have been imposed on us from the outside, without critical examination. Whether we still support certain ideologies, norms, and values, at the first step, we negate our ideologies and values temporarily in order to open up new possibilities of change, to test their validity and to avoid possible mistakes by unexamined ideologies, if they are not valid.

The negative aspects of unexamined ideology are well described in Marx as a false consciousness. Marx understood ideology as "the corruption of reason by interest."[4] In his ideas, ideology is a false consciousness of both victims and the privileges of the existing social orders that accept and justify particular interests of the privileged in a society unconsciously.[5] Thus, Marx analyzed ideology in society as "a rational justification of the status quo, or the unexamined theory behind an immoral praxis."[6] Facing this type of ideology, we should negate it since it limits any potential for

---

4) Pieris, 26.
5) *Ibid.*
6) *Ibid.*

change. This process is similar to filtering out false ideologies in ourselves by being self-critical.

Although we may be able to negate ideologies, norms, and values in the process of the hermeneutic negation, we need to be selective about negating more fundamental ones that deny and prevent the Christian love of others and to struggle with them more seriously in reality. For example, when ideologies structurally facilitate the hatred and negligence of others such as what happens in racism, sexism, oppression, and manipulation, we need the necessary tools to negate such ideologies and values inside of us and our society with reasonable expectations based on our limitations.

As ideologies and values tend to support status quo, it is more difficult for us to challenge them than to accept them. It is difficult because we have benefited from the ideologies and because the privileged try to perpetuate them with socio-economic and political hegemony.[7] Thus, we should be courageous enough to give up our interests and to confront

---

7) Otto Maduro, *Religion and Social Conflicts,* 124.

possible oppressions from the privilege. The concept of the hermeneutic negation as the first step of doing ethics helps us think that comforting values and ideologies that are favorable to the privileged are something that should be ethically confronted and denied, demanding courage, at the beginning of our doing ethics. Such ideologies are not something that we struggle and suffer with endlessly, but rather, are these that we negate and discard in order to move on to next step of doing ethics.

> *Example-Step#1: Hermeneutic Negation:*
>
> *At this point, I do not accept this statement and interpret as it is described. Rather I negate the negative influences from the outside at least temporarily. Thus, I will negate the negative ideology in the statement regarding the hermeneutic negation as follow, "~~You, Koreans, are sneaky people.~~ You do not look at my eyes when you speak to me."*

The second step I identify as hermeneutic affirmation. This is an affirmation of my identity and being itself, and, and the negation of negating myself imposed by social ideologies and values that are outside of me. In reality, this can also be selective according to priorities, which are focused on the negation of ideologies and values that deny and prevent Christian love of the self, and on full acceptance of one's being and the self as it is. Also, this step comprises a critical reflection of my self and the ideology that I embrace, and encompasses my understanding of myself and my ideology that are negatively influenced by the ideologies of the privileged.

For example, I had a discussion with a Korean American person about Church music and particular instruments that our Korean immigrant church could purchase. While discussing contemporary church music, I discovered that he considered himself only as American and did not like to be asked for help as a Korean by other Koreans based on his appearance. However, it seemed ironic that he still attended a Korean immigrant church, while trying to distance himself from the Koreans. Also, when he talked about contemporary musical trends of America and frequently referred to the American Church, he focused on the white American Church and its music only, which are the standard of American church for him. Thus, he identified himself only with the standard white Americans and white American Church. In my thinking, his ideological references and values about himself deny a part of his being and self that he cannot change. He does not want to accept that he is a second generation Korean American. Instead, he wants to accept only a part of himself as American.

An additional concern for the hermeneutic affirmation is the need to accept difference, diversity, and the uniqueness of our selves. Because such difference and uniqueness have been considered as inferiority, we should critically re-examine our ideologies, and thus, selectively affirm parts of our being as body, skin colors, culture, language, and identity that have been stigmatized by ideologies of the privileged. With our own hermeneutic lenses, Christian love of the self can be understood as our acceptance and affirmation of our beings and selves as they are. The hermeneutic affirmation can provide an opportunity for the marginalized and the voiceless to raise up their voices and share something genuine out of themselves with others. In addition, the hermeneutic affirmation can help people to build up their own ideologies, values, and norms, which are minimized from the influences of the oppressive ideologies of the privileged.

> *Example-Step #2: Hermeneutic Affirmation*
>
> *At this step, I affirm my culture and identity in the previous statement. "~~You, Koreans, are sneaky people.~~ You do not look at my eyes when you speak to me (And I affirm this behavior as my cultural identity)."*

The third step is to expand our own experiences, values, norms, ideologies towards the construction of our new experience which, in fact, overlaps common ones with others. By sharing our experiences with others,' we can find the necessity of the expansion of our ideologies as anticipated in the arguments of Manheim. Manheim introduced the concept of "the particular" and "the total"[8] in explaining the meaning of ideologies. According to Manheim, we often use "the particular conception of ideology" when we are suspicious of "the ideas and representations advanced by our opponent."[9] Such ideas and representations are "regarded as more or less conscious disguises of the real nature of a situation, the true recognition of which would not be in accord with his interest."[10] The ranges of distortions vary from conscious lies to unconscious disguises, and "from calculated attempts to dupe others to self-deception."[11] The problem of the particular understanding of ideology is that it is limited to a one-sidedness that reveals a negative aspect. Thus, it does not provide us with comprehensive conceptions of ideology.

Considering this deficit, Manheim, therefore, suggests the

---

8) Karl Manheim, *Ideology and Utopia* (New York: Harcourt, Brace & World, INC., 1936), 49.

9) *Ibid.*

10) *Ibid.*

11) *Ibid.*

second understanding of ideology that is called the total conception of ideology in order to overcome such one-sidedness. The total conception of ideology is understood as "the ideology of an age or of a concrete historico-social group, e.g. of a class, when we are concerned with the characteristics and composition of the total structure of the mind of this epoch or of this group."[12] This understanding dials with a broader notion in which Manheim tried to analyze and interpret an era or a group on a much large scale. In doing so, he expanded the construction of his hermeneutics considerably.

The differences between these two understandings are that the total conception of ideology focuses on the totality of the structure of a social group in a given historical context, while the particular conception of ideology deals with an aspect of personal assertions related with the psychology of interests of the opponents.[13] Ideology remains particular

---

12) *Ibid.*, 49-50.
13) *Ibid.*, 51-52.

when it is used as an analytical tool that reveals the ideas of the opponent. For example, "the word ideology is used as a weapon by the proletariat against the dominant group."[14] However, the pitfall of the particular understanding of ideology is that it does not reflect one's own position. If the particular understanding does not question one's own position, and thus, regards it as a corpus of absolute norms by which to interpret and analyze the opponent's ideas, there will be no advancement of ideas.[15]

According to Manheim, the analyst uses the total conception of ideology to subject not only the opponent's perspective, but also to expand all of the possible perspectives, including one's own view.[16] This self-critical analysis may bring about the uncertainty of universal norms, however, "It is precisely our uncertainty which brings us a good deal closer to reality than was possible in former periods which had

---

14) *Ibid.*, 66.
15) *Ibid.*, 68.
16) *Ibid.*, 68-69.

faith in the absolute."[17]

Manheim did not believe that uncertainty from our self-critical analysis would necessarily lead to relativism. Rather, in the total conception of ideology, people would be guided to relationism, not to relativism.[18] Manheim believes, "Relationism signifies merely that all of the elements of meaning in a given situation have reference to one another and derive their significance from this reciprocal inter-relationship in a given frame of thought."[19]

Universal norms in relationism are grounded in the historical situations of people and secure "the relationship of all partial knowledge and its component elements to the larger body of meaning, and ultimately to the structure of historical reality."[20] In other words, they continuously expand and validate their meanings through the interactions with partial historical knowledge and experiences until they

---

17) *Ibid.,* 75.
18) *Ibid.,* 75-76.
19) *Ibid.,* 76.
20) *Ibid.,* 77.

hold more general and universal meanings that are enough to become references for conflicting cases. Thus, when historical situations change, the universal norms that have come out of and are used for the specific time and situation dynamically change.

According to Manheim, it is questionable for us to seek the immutable and absolute ideas and norms. Manheim argues, "It is not primarily the man of action who seeks the absolute and immutable, but rather it is he who wishes to induce others to hold on to the status quo because he feels comfortable and smug under conditions as they are."[21] In other words, Manheim argues that the privileges would try to make their temporal social conditions as absolute orders and ideas in order to have stable chance to be benefited.[22] By seeking universal norms that interact with historical situations, Manheim tries to construct a general ideology that promotes social change, rather than the status quo. He tries

---

21) *Ibid.*, 78.
22) *Ibid.*

to reveal the truth, rather than conceal it.

The construction of universal norms in relationism is possible only when we test every idea of its relevance and validity with reality, including our own understanding of reality that is also to be questioned and revised.[23] As we continue to expand and test the norms of our analysis based on historical realities, the differences of conflicting ideologies may be reduced to "different modes of experiencing the 'same' reality.[24] In this process of assimilating different perspectives, our understanding of ideology will become more comprehensive.[25]

In the pursuit of the total conception of ideology, Manheim believed that we will never be satisfied with particular perspectives, but will continuously seek to understand and analyze them from a more inclusive and comprehensive context.[26] According to Manheim, totality represents "the

---

23) *Ibid.*, 87–88.
24) *Ibid.*, 88–89.
25) *Ibid.*, 92.
26) *Ibid.*, 94.

continuous process of the expansion of knowledge, and has as its goal not the achievement of a super-temporally valid conclusion but the broadest possible extension of our horizon of vision."[27] He believed that we can overcome the contemporary crises only "through the gradual extension and deepening of newly -won insights and through careful advances in the direction of control."[28]

Despite Manheim's endeavor to construct the universal norms in the total conception of ideology, it is not clear whether he was successful or not because we are barely transcendental with degrees of limitation. In order to make his concept of universal norms applicable to every realm and situation, Manheim seems to block out fundamental notions of immutability and absoluteness in the concept of universality by making it subjective in relation to history and various types of criticism. In other words, his concept of universality is subjective in relation to continuous changes in

---

27) *Ibid.*, 94-95.
28) *Ibid.*, 96.

history, but remains objective in relation to universal norms at the same time. By using the term, universality, we are moving further into the realm of abstraction thus diminishing the effectiveness, resulting from concrete experiences and realities. Additionally, the value with overlapping experiences is significantly diminished.

However, as we speculate on the normativity in our daily lives, we find out that it is often subjective to our own interests, and how difficult it is for us to be absolutely objective in judgments and actions and whether our norms are continuously changing or not. Therefore, we should allow for subjectivities in both the changeability and normativity of universality, while preventing this argument from falling into relativism.

One of the practical ways to deal with the issues of particularity, totality, and universality is to construct overlapping common norms and values for our ethical life and to focus on the process itself, rather than on the result of the process. We start from our own historical realities, subjective experiences, and particularities, which are fundamental in our understanding of the world. However, at the same time, we should try to overcome our narrow one-sidedness by expanding and building up a common overlapping basis, sharing our experiences, ideas, and values with others. Such overlapping of common ideologies, norms, and values are not objective universal norms in themselves. Rather, they are continuously tested and expanded subjective norms that try to seek broader applications.

At this point, I especially want to emphasize the importance of the oppressed in the construction of common overlapping grounds of dialogue as they have the potential of experiencing self-determination resulting from the previous two hermeneutic steps. Because the oppressed traditionally have been more silenced and marginalized, they have considerable experiences to bring to the table of discussion. At the moment of sharing with others, we have the opportunity to share the intersecting experiences of both oppression and self-affirmation, and can acknowledge particular overlapping common experiences, ideologies, norms, and values. Such intersection of common experiences and ideas can unite us by providing common ground to share. In the process of finding the common ground with other oppressed people, we may expand our hermeneutic perspectives and understandings of our experiences and ideologies, and use them as norms and values in our doing ethics.

> *Example-Step #3: Hermeneutic Expansion and Examination Through Dialogue with The Oppressed*
>
> *At this step, I will expand and test my affirmed ideas from my experiences through discussions with other, especially, the poor, the oppressed, the silenced, and the marginalized.*
>
> *For example, my affirmation of my own ideas, culture, and identity in the statement, "~~You, Koreans, are sneaky people.~~ <u>You do not look at my eyes when you speak to me (And I affirm this behavior as my cultural identity.)</u> will be examined through discussion with others. Through my experiences with other Korean elders, I find that this attitude is praiseworthy by*

> *them. Then, how do others understand this attitude? How do young Koreans or other people in different cultures understand this? Especially, how can people who suffered from racism or Koreans who suffered from this specific statement respond to my affirmation? Through this process, I expand and examine my affirmation through my experiences and discussions with others.*

The fourth step of the hermeneutic spiral is to test and re-affirm the expanded common ideologies, norms, and values in our praxis. Our shared ideologies, norms, and values are tested at the level of dialogue where they can be re-tested and re-examined at the level of praxis. By doing so, they can be refined and re-affirmed in order to become a new and expanded common ideology with shared norms and values, reflecting the present realities of our living world.

In addition, the praxis of our intersecting common ideology, norms, and values can reshape our understanding as well. In other words, our understanding of ideology and its praxis are interactional, and thus, influence each other in molding, refinement, and construction. On the one hand, our common ideologies, norms, and values affect the practice of our morality. On the other hand, they are shaped in our ethical practice and actions at the same time. The outcomes of these interactions should be re-examined from the very first step of a hermeneutic spiral because of the tendency to seek self-interests in ourselves and in the social groups to which we belong and with which we identify. If we follow through the process of the hermeneutic spiral, our perspectives, ideologies, values, and norms will/should be expanded towards broader overlapping common ones.

Example-Step #4: Hermeneutic Expansion and Re-examination Through Praxis

"~~You, Koreans, are sneaky people.~~ You do not look at my eyes when you speak to me (And I affirm this behavior as my cultural identity and I will help others understand the importance of my own culture.)

At this level, I practice my affirmed ideas and learning from the third step. Through my praxis, I am more certain that my conclusion from dialogue with others affirms my attitude. In addition, I work together with the oppressed to convince people who have cultural prejudices against Koreans, to challenge and change their racist attitudes.

With my expanded and confirmed conclusion, I go back to the question at the first step. Then, I test again if the original statement and my negation against the specific ideology within it If I am right to negate the negative statement to me through the process, I expand my reflections whether I can understand the reasons why others have such racist attitude and ideas toward me and other Koreans. Then, I go to the second step of affirmation with this practical knowledge. By this continuous reflection and expansion like a spiral, I seek the overlapping common ground for interpretation of the world.

3. Application of A Hermeneutic Spiral

In this section, I will analyze a conflict situation of that occurred in South Korea to illustrate my concept of a hermeneutic spiral. An ideology plays an important role in our decision-making process. Ideology provides moral agents with a system of understanding of the world that is fundamental in the process of our decision-making. Furthermore, it enables us to be self-critical and to have universal references in relationship with reality that are used for our ethical analysis and evaluation. On the other hand, persons in life situations are both moral agents and subjects. The ideology of the moral person in the interaction with realities in life situations serve as the determinants for an ethical life. Let me begin with a brief summary of a recent political situation in Korea.

Recently, Korean opinion was divided on the issue on whether the National Security Law (NSL) should be abolished or not. National Security Law was originally instituted on December 1, 1948, immediately falling after the establishment of the Republic of Korea (South Korea) that achieved independence from Japan. Originally, the purpose of the NSL was to establish order for Korean society by suppressing the riots generated by various ideologies. Soon after, however, it was used to oppress every political group whose voice was against the government. For example, more than 100,000 people were arrested and jailed and more than one hundred parties and social organizations were dissolved in 1949 alone.

The NSL was continuously used and amended to oppress the Korean people who had different opinions contrary to those of the government or who were believed to be against the dictatorship of the Korean government. Especially, after the Korean War, the NSL was combined with the Anti-Communism Law that defined every socialist nation an enemy of South Korea. Thus, any type of political expressions and any form of journalisms that were perceived as being the government were censored and oppressed. As a result, some people were fabricated as spies of North Korea and were executed under the NSL. Many others including politicians, students, and labor union members were persecuted as communists.

Still, the NSL continues to be used to secure existing order in the Korean society. Although the progressive government party that currently is the majority in the Congress has tried to abolish the NSL as late as last year, 2004, they have failed to do so due to the objection of the minor opposition party that comprises the privileged group of the elites and members of the former party for a long time.

The problem in the issue of NSL is that, while the government tries to abolish it, the majority of Koreans seem to be against its abolishment. According to recent surveys, about 60% of Korean people think that NSL should be either preserved or amended in part. Only about 30-35% of Koreans believed should be abolished.[29] Furthermore, both the Constitutional Court and the Supreme Court stated in August and September, 2004, that the NSL is in agreement with the Constitution of Korea and is necessary in consideration of the military and political situation of the Korean peninsula.[30]

---

29) http://news.go.kr/warp/webapp/issue/poll/list. Accessed on October 1, 2011.

Considering the socio-political situations existing in Korea, certain questions need to be raised: Despite the fact that the NSL has been used to oppress the basic human rights of the Korean people, why do many Koreans still support the maintenance of the NSL? That very law has victimized many Koreans who have struggled for justice, but why is the majority against the abolishment of an inhumane law? We have learned that the privileged who are the minority pursue the status quo in order to guarantee their interests. However, why do the majority of people who are vulnerable to the inhumane law still support it?

In the first place, the experiences of evil in the modern history of Korea have played an important role for Koreans in making ethical judgment on the issue of the NSL. Koreans have experienced the instability of society because of the results from Japanese colonization and the Korean War. In particular, many Koreans have lost their property and the

---

30) http://news.go.kr/warp/webapp/issue/news.
   Accessed on October 1, 2011.

lives of the **thousand** of families during and after the Korean War. Koreans have experienced the evils of war caused by North Korean communists that have resulted in one of the most tragic periods in Korean history. After the truce of the Korean War, there were several occasions of alleged infiltration of armed agents from North Korea. Allegations of civilian communist spies were often fabricated by the South Korean military regime in order to maintain the political power. As a result, many South Koreans continue to be concerned about the break out of another war on the Korean peninsula.

Ivone Gebara illumines us on the importance of experience. She finds the starting point of her theology from women's experience of evil in everyday life. Especially, she listens to the stories of women in Latin America, because of "the experience of poor and oppressed women... is more silent and others."[31] Gebara argues that understanding, or, interpretation of evil is not so simple as people believe.

---

31) Gebara, 14.

Rather, she asserts, "Good and evil are mixed up and feed off one another."[32] She believes that good and evil are intermingled in our daily lives, enlighten us to understand each other's nature by comparison and contrast, even by the fact of their coexistence. Evil seems to be everywhere in our lives[33] and "one evil must be destroyed by another evil to become a good."[34] Evil and good are like something like comes and goes, and comes again which, in the end, will lead to the triumph of good.[35]

In the minds of many Koreans, especially those who experienced the Korean War, North Korean communists are understood as the cause of evil because they started the Korean War. The impact of their experience of evil in the Korean War was so strong that they still fear the North Korean government and its presence. Because of the experience of the evils of the Korean War, many Koreans have

---

32) *Ibid.*,44.
33) *Ibid.*,56.
34) *Ibid.*,27.
35) *Ibid.*,179.

shaped an ideology of anti-communism, anti-socialism, and of national security. Whatever resembles their perception of communism, they seem abhor even talking about the issue or thinking about it.

They seem to believe that the exercise of force by the government is justified. They justify even the oppression of basic human rights of South Koreans by the government and believe it is permitted and even necessary in order to protect a democratic South Korea from the communist North Korea. Following their thinking, it seems that the greater evil of communism can be and should be prevented by the lesser evil of the NSL.

However, the life situation of Korean people has been changed since the Korean War and immutable ideology that does not correspond to historical situation tends to reinforce the status quo as Manheim argued.[36] Also, holding onto a particular ideology does not provide a society with the advancement of ideas. In other words, as long as the South

---

36) Manheim, 78.

Koreans adhere to the ideology of anti-communism, they cannot be critical of their own ideas. Thus further discussions with people who have different ideas are consequently blocked. Even though the experiences of evil in the Korean War were so great, South Koreans should respond to the changes of their contemporary life situation in order to make an ethical decision.

As I have discussed, the ideologies of anti-communism, anti-socialism, and of national security are often manipulated by anti-democratic military regimes in South Korea. The regimes created and programmed such ideologies in order to maximize their interests, holding the status quo of Korean society. The privileged who are the minority of the society have been able to manipulate the thinking of the majority Korean people through social conflicts, unjust exercise of force and laws. The ideologies of anti-communism, anti- socialism, and of national security as well as of the development that was later added to justify the evils of forces by the government have prevented many Koreans from critical self- reflection, and silenced the voices of the oppressed and the marginalized.

Often, religions in Korean society have justified such ideologies, or, were silent to the unjust ideologies. For example, most Christians passively accepted the evils under the NSL, or actively justified and propagandized the ideologies. Christians who have struggled for justice against NSL have been in the minority. Maduro explains how religion functions in relation with ideology and social change.

According to Maduro, religion has a double function that both preserves the hegemony of the dominant minority, and yet, challenges and changes their dominance. According to him, religion is not something that is universally situated in society. His presumption is, "Every religion is situated in a specific mode of production" and "The activity of any religion is limited and orientated by the specific mode of production within which it functions."[37] Thus, religion and reli-

---

37) Otto Maduro, *Religion and Social Conflicts* (Maryknoll, NY: Orbis Books, 1982), 46.

gious activity are limited by their own particularity.

In our society, a mode of production, a power of society, is asymmetrical and belongs to a certain minority rather than a vast majority.[38] The minority with their asymmetrical power control the majority for their own sake. Religion, in this sense, is an effective tool and system for the minority to exercise their asymmetrical power in order to preserve their hegemony over the majority. The tendency of religion is to support "the maintenance of the internal harmonious equilibrium of a society."[39]

However, Maduro points out another aspect of the function of religion. According to him, "Religion does not always perform purely conservative functions with respect to conflictive social relationships of dominance."[40] Because religion is located and directed by specific realities of social groups, subordinate social groups can transform the existing

---

38) *Ibid.*,48.

39) *Ibid.*,118.

40) *Ibid.*,136.

social structures if they can "construct a religious worldview independent of, different from, and in opposition to the dominant worldview in their society."[41]

Maduro explains that aspects as below.

> The potential revolutionary function of certain groups of clergy is more likely to be actualized where (1) the subordinate sectors linked to them make religious demands whose content is markedly autonomous and antihegemonic, and (2) where the church itself is the seat of new theological developments favorable to the autonomy of subordinate classes.[42]

Korean churches have performed both functions in modern history. However, the majority of Korean churches have followed ideologies of anti-communism and national security and, thus, have helped the privileged by maintaining the status quo. The majority of Korean churches have pro-

---

41) *Ibid.*,137.
42) *Ibid.*,144.

vided many symbols and narratives for the ideologies of anti-communism, of national security, and of development. Thus, marginalized and victimized people have suffered from such ideologies and the NSL.

In fact, Gebara's arguments on evil reveal to us how Latin women who are poor and marginalized have had to suffer from the evils of social systems. With new perspectives, she criticizes and analyzes theology that has been dominated by men. According to her, Christianity has been violent and justified violence against people, especially, women.[43] For her, religious symbols and languages represent maleness and authoritatively force women to be obedient to traditional patriarchal traditions of Christianity.[44] Within this system, "God and Christological models hinder the self-determination of persons, especially of women."[45]

Gebara's theology gives us new insights and challenges

---

43) Ivone Gebara, *Out of the Depths* (Minneapolis: Fortress Press, 2002), 104.

44) *Ibid.,* 106.

45) *Ibid.,* 107.

us to reinterpret the problems of evil in our daily lives, especially, among the poor and women especially those who are marginalized. She argues that theology should be grounded in the concrete situation of our daily lives, and in the solidarity of the marginalized people, especially women who are poor and marginalized. When theology can connect the daily sufferings and struggles of the women to themes of the salvation and resurrection, it will provide norms of justice and hope.

Most Korean churches have not developed a new frame for a worldview against that of thee dominant. While many Korean people have suffered from the experience of evil in the Korean War and following the violence and oppression by the military regime, Korean churches have been unable to provide the total conception of ideology that would challenge and change the oppressive situations of Korea. Thus, most Korean Christians are unconscious or falsely conscious of social realities. As a result, they remain in ideology of anti-communism, of national security, and of a development that is oppressive to both others and themselves.

Rather, most Korean churches justify violence against people and support status quo. For example, they did not to listen to the voices of the poor and the marginalized, especially of women who were silenced at home, in church, and in society for a long time. They could not connect to the daily sufferings and struggles of male and female to themes of the salvation and resurrection as Gebara argues. Thus, they have been unable to provide norms of justice and hope for Korean Christians.

Without the development of a new ideology, Korean people are still influenced and programmed by the dominant ideologies that are created and recreated through media, culture, religious symbols and narratives, as well as laws by the privileged. The privileged minority has been able to control the majority through ideology and social, cultural, religious, and political norms and values that represent hegemonic political power. The ideologies generated by the privileged minority have educated and programmed the majority of the Korean people, and have become false ideologies seemingly representing the welfare and best interest of the majority. Thus, the majority of Koreans have supported the NSL without critical self-reflection in the particular ideologies.

In this sense, it is not always true that the opinions of the majority are valid even in a democratic society. If the majority of groups do not develop an ideology that can liberate themselves, there remains the possibility of oppression, manipulation, and the suffering of people. In order to overcome this problem, Korean people need to develop a new ideology that would challenge and change society.

For the construction of a new ideology, comprising norms, and values for Korean society, we may apply the concept of a hermeneutic spiral. In the first step of the hermeneutic negation, Korean churches especially should be able to negate fundamental ideologies that deny and prevent the Christian love of others. From the realities of the Korean people, tools such as the NSL that have been used to oppress the people who sought for democracy and against the military regime need to be changed. In this sense, the ideology of anti-communism must also be boldly negated though there has been the experience of evil among the older generation of Korean people. Because the ideology of anti-communism has been used to maintain the status quo and oppression of the Korean people, it no longer has validity to become the overlapping common ideology.

In the second step of the hermeneutic affirmation, Koreans and Korean churches need to affirm their personhood and negate the social structures that have negated such self-determination and survival. In the second process, Koreans should accept the difference, diversity, and uniqueness of themselves as well as other Koreans. "You and I" may have different ideas and values, however, they should be accepted as genuine parts of themselves, rather than something inferior to those who are privileged. Especially, the oppressed and marginalized Koreans should accept themselves as genuine beings, not inferior beings determined by the ideologies of the privileged. The marginalized who were unable to speak up, despite supporting the abolishment of the NSL, may acknowledge now that they have been right to do so but need the encouragement and empowerment to effect it. In addition, if they have been thinking that they are unable to abolish the NSL under the demonizing force of the privileged for the status quo, they can acknowledge that their tiny efforts to change Korean society may result in actual reformation.

In the third step, Koreans may expand their understanding of ideologies, experiences, values, and norms on NSL by sharing them with others, especially with the oppressed. They will find out whether their own understandings of the NSL have been too narrow or one-sided. Especially, those who have supported the NSL under the ideology of anti-communism and the experience of the evil can share their experiences and ideas with those of the oppressed who have suffered from the NSL. Because they started "doing ethics" by hermeneutically negating the fundamental ideology of the NSL, at least temporarily, Koreans can test and examine the validity of previous ideologies that they have by sharing their own affirmed ideas and experiences. In the process of testing and expanding their affirmed experiences and ideas through sharing with others, Koreans can find overlapping common norms, values, experiences, and ideologies that can be used as broader norms for the reformation of Korean society.

As the fourth step, Koreans have intersecting common ideologies and norms and can take action in order to realize their norms and values in Korean society. For those who share the ideas of supporting the abolishment of the NSL may actually work in their daily lives. In the process of actualization of their overlapping ideologies and norms on the issue of the NSL, Koreans can examine, change, and refine their previous ideas and understandings of the NSL. Especially, Korean churches may develop new alternative ideologies for Christians, based on Christian love of the self and others among the overlapping common values and

norms, and expand and test them in the process of a hermeneutic spiral.

Then, what kinds of values and norms will be included
in the overlapping common norms for Korean society? What
would help Koreans, especially Korean Christians, make
ethical decision and action? Gutierrez provides us with some
clues to respond to the questions. According to Gutierrez,
peace, justice, and life are important theme for which we
need to search.[46] Also, he argues that what theology deals
with is not an abstraction but "real, living persons."[47] Thus,
the theological task confirms the superiority of human being
over material objects.[48]

In the process of our ethical-decision making, we should
take these themes as norms on which to reflect. Ideologies
that abstract realities of everyday life and contradict peace,
justice, and life would not nurture the person to become a

---

46) Gustavo Gutiérrez, *The Truth Shall Make You Free* (Maryknoll:
    Orbis Boosk, 1990), 75.

47) *Ibid.*

48) *Ibid.*

moral agent and subject. Rather, only ideologies that promote these themes will help the person become a moral agent and subject in relationality and responsibility with the social realities of our lives.

To become the person as a moral agent and subject emphasizes the importance of conscience in ethical decision-making process. Isasi-Diaz finds that conscience plays an important role in the everyday lives of Hispanic women, and thus, tries to enhance their moral developments. Under oppressive circumstances, conscience helps the person to aware of oneself as a moral agent and subject. Isasi-Diaz understands conscience as "the agent herself as morally conscious, and since consciousness is constitutive of the human person as agent, the formation of moral consciousness has to do with enabling the process of conscientization of the person."[49] One of the significant aspects about the process of conscientization is "the importance of praxis in its rela-

---

49) Ada Maria Isasi-Diaz, *The Power of the Poor in History* (Maryknoll: Orbis Books, 1984), 162.

tionship to liberation."[50]

In consideration of the issue of the NSL, the emphasis of conscientization of the person and the praxis for liberation are crucial. The majority of Korean people who believed the maintenance of the NSL due to specific ideologies created by the privileged are called to the process of conscientization now. In some sense, it has been natural for them to support the ideologies of the status quo because they did not participate in the praxis for liberation. Without praxis for liberation, the majority of Korean people have supported ideologies that justified oppression and manipulation of the marginalized and the poor. Without praxis, they have accepted and justified ideologies that negated basic human rights and have been unable to realize that they are moral agents in everyday lives.

The concept of a hermeneutic spiral may help Koreans to critically reflect on their ideologies and test them in the process of expanding them to overlapping common ideolo-

---

50) *Ibid.*, 161.

gies and norms. Moreover, a hermeneutic spiral necessitates the importance of praxis as a part of the ethical process. Thus, the concept of a hermeneutic spiral certainly has the potential to promote social changes in Korean society and in other contexts by those who employ it.

4. Conclusion

Ideology plays an important role in our ethical decision-making process and action. As a frame of understanding the world, ideology provides specific meanings and functions with people. As a result, it may provide references for either conflict or peaceful resolution among people. In my belief, the ideology that constructs overlapping common references and norms is possible in the process of a hermeneutic spiral. It also provides broader perspectives and norms for our ethical decision-making process as well as nurtures us to become moral agents and subjects.

In the case of Korean society that is divided by the issue of the NSL, ideologies have played critical roles in ethical decision-making process and in their actions of Korean people. Many Koreans have been manipulated and controlled, not only by the experience of evils related to the Korean War, but also by the created ideologies of anti-communism, anti-socialism, and national security. Without praxis for liberation, many Koreans, including the majority of Korean churches, accept and justify the ideologies that have oppressed many other Koreans who have struggled for justice and liberation. Without praxis and conscientization, they have not listened to the voices of or seen the realities of others who have experienced the evils of oppression and deprivation of basic human rights. Thus, they have supported oppressive ideologies of the status quo created by the privileged minority.

For most Koreans, it is time to develop a new ideology that promotes justice, and peace for the lives of all persons.

With new understandings of the world that changes continuously, they need to construct a new ideology with accompanying norms, and values that continuously interact with the realities of changing history. The development of such an ideology that would promote justice and peace for the lives of all persons would help Koreans become and act as moral agents and subjects, made possible through the process of a hermeneutic spiral.

Bibliography

Curran, Charles. *Moral Theology: A Continuing Journey.* Notre Dame: University of Notre Dame Press, 1982.

_____. *Directions in Fundamental Moral Theology.* Notre Dame: University 7 of Notre Dame Press, 1985.

Gebara, Ivone. *Out of the Depths.* Minneapolis: Fortress Press, 2002.

Gutiérrez, Gustavo. *The Power of the Poor in History.* Maryknoll: Orbis Books, 1984.

_____. *The Truth Shall Make You Free.* Maryknoll: Orbis Boosk, 1990.

Isasi-Diaz, Ada Maria. *Mujerista Theology.* Maryknoll: Orbis Books, 1996.

_____. *En La Lucha.* Minneapolis: Fortress Press, 2004.

Maduro, Otto. *Religion and Social Conflicts.* Maryknoll, NY: Orbis Books, 1982.

Manheim, Karl. *Ideology and Utopia.* New York: Harcourt, Brace & World, INC., 1936.

Pieris, Aloysius. *An Asian Theology of Liberation.* Maryknoll, Orbis Books, 1988.

Segundo, Juan Luis. *The Liberation of Theology.* Maryknoll: Orbis Books, 1982.

Smith, Dorothy E. *The Everyday World as Problematic.* Boston: Northeastern University Press, 1987.

Troeltsch, Ernst. *The Social Teaching.* Vol. 1. Harper, NY, 1960.

Walker, Margaret. *Moral Understanding.* NY: Rutledge, 1998.

Internet Resources:

http://news.go.kr/warp/webapp/issue/news. Accessed on Oct.1, 2011.

http://news.go.kr/warp/webapp/issue/poll/list. Accessed on Oct.1, 2011.

II

Toward Sustainable Justice

1. Introduction

Why do we still speak of justice today? We cry out for justice where the presence of poverty, inequality, violence, and forms of discrimination such as racism and sexism exist. Justice needs to be realized in the presence of such evil and injustice.

The presumption in our cry is that justice is a value and a goal of society. Justice is a value identified as the good, while injustice is identified as a form of evil. We pursue and define a good society through the value of justice. Thus, justice becomes a norm when we apply it into our individual and social lives. In the continuation of the pursuit of justice as a goal, justice is understood as a process.

However, in contemporary society it becomes more difficult to achieve a social consensus of what justice means and how justice should be achieved, because of the complexities of social relations and structures. As contemporary society becomes more diverse and pluralistic, a broader spectrum of voices and ideas seem to spring from the dynamics of contemporary society. Therefore, it becomes more difficult to define justice and to find appropriate methods on which to frame and construct systems for justice as they are needed in complex society.

This essay is, therefore, an *attempt* to provide a variety of descriptive definitions of justice in contemporary society, rather than develop a comprehensive definition. In the process of my attempt to develop my own concept of justice, I attempt to answer to following questions, "What is the starting point in developing a definition of justice and where should it go? How can we achieve justice?"

To this purpose, I will illustrate problems of some theories of justice, and explain important elements for the construction of my own definition of justice. Critical to this task are discussions of the elements in justice which are parts of my journey to answer these questions. In my last part of this essay, I construct my own concept of justice using previously discussed elements.

I present my concept of justice as *sustainable* justice, or, justice of *living and growing together the vulnerable*. I am aware of the limitations of labeling justice as such. However, I believe that this attempt would provide us with a new perspective of understanding the concept of justice.

2. Starting Points

Where should justice start and where should it go? Why should we[1] start from a specific point? Christian ethics challenges us to see the reality of the poor in speaking of justice. From theological perspectives, God is the deliverer of the poor.[2] In the Bible, God demonstrates the preferential love for the poor and the marginalized. In the deliberative works of God, the poor, the powerless, and the marginalized are at the center of God's concern and care. These Christian traditions of liberation illustrate that we should start the discussion of justice from the reality of the poor.

The problem is, however, that we often neglect the Bible verses that speak for the poor. God's concerns and preference for the poor are blurred and erased by our own interests when we read the Bible. Thus, it is imperative that we focus on the reality of the poor and redefine our priorities, once we learn the genuine biblical perspectives. Jim Wallis, a social activist in Washington, understands it as "a matter

---

1) By this, I mean, most of the Christians living in the wealthy countries such as the United States and the Western European countries.

2) Jim Wallis, *The Soul of Politics* (A Harvest Book: New York, 1995), 180.

of conversion."[3] He insists, "To place the reality of the poor at the center of our attention will require a fundamental change in priorities and direction."[4] In his views, our conversion to the Bible is tested not by our words that we engage, but by our actions that we live.

Then, how can we restore and convert to the biblical perspectives, if it is our tendency to pursue our own interests? Moreover, do we not try to disconnect ourselves from the reality of the poor in our daily lives? It seems that most individuals want to keep a safe distance from the poor, dividing ourselves from our neighbors.[5] We pretend to know the problems of the poor, but actually, we do not choose to understand the reality of the poor, nor do we respond to the reality of the poor.

Wallis argues that compassion is a necessary factor for us to engage. According to him, "The word *compassion* literally

---

3) *Ibid.*

4) *Ibid.*

5) *Ibid.*,193-194.

means 'to suffer with,' to put yourself in someone else's position, to walk for a little while in her or his shoes."[6] Thus, compassion is an essential component for us to relate with the poor, breaking down the barriers between us and our neighbors.

However, in order to have compassion for the poor, it is important to persist a careful listening to the story of the poor. Wallis argues, "Hearing one another's stories is the beginning of new understanding and the foundation of compassionate action."[7] That is, listening to the stories of the poor enlightens us to see the connection between us and the poor, and enables us to understand and to act for the poor. Thus, listening to the poor is a kind of revelation in capturing the true meaning of the Gospel as well as a source of empowerment for the transformation of our lives for compassionate action to follow the Gospel.

John O'Brien, a social activist and ethicist, also agrees

---

6) *Ibid.*,193.
7) *Ibid.*, 194.

with the necessity to centralize the reality of the poor, and to have a hermeneutic dialogue with the poor as a therapeutic way to self-correct contemporary theology. His arguments have two fundamental assumptions: One is "the acquisition of the perspective of the poor," and another is "an involvement in the struggle of the oppressed," which enables Christian theology to interpret the true meaning of Christian faith with "a privileged hermeneutical perspective."[8] Through this hermeneutical perspective, O'Brien tries to analyze and interpret "a consequence of structure of injustice and oppression,"[9] and to speak of an option for the poor that means "the choice to attempt to love all in and through a partisan love for the oppressed."[10]

O'Brien argues further that all human structures are described by power relations that result in marginalization and oppression.[11] Thus, the issue of the poor is not a local issue,

---

8) John O'Brien, *Theology and the Option for the Poor* (The Liturgical Press: Collegeville, 1992), 8.
9) *Ibid.*
10) *Ibid.*,10.

but a universal issue to which theology should make options for them. O'Brien believes that our conversion to the poor, through theological praxis, in our experience with the poor and through the process of conversation with the poor, will facilitate the development of defining the hermeneutical perspective of the options for the poor.[12] In so doing, a therapeutic role and the discovery of a new quality of human solidarity can be realized.[13]

In summary, the discussion of justice in Christian ethics must find its fundamental basis in the context of the poor. The reality of the poor requires that our understanding of justice should be directed toward the options for the poor which is a universal mandate for theories of justice. That is, our understanding of justice should include a "conversion" to the poor that means to centralize the poor in our lives with a preferential love for them, and compassion that connects

---

11) *Ibid.*,59.
12) *Ibid.*,159.
13) *Ibid.*

us with the poor by being in solidarity with them. Conversion and compassion are possible only when we listen to the stories of the poor, and join the dialogue with the poor with reflection and praxis. Through the process of our dialogue with the poor, we will have a hermeneutical perspective that will generate self-correction of our understanding of justice as well as of theology. With the hermeneutical perspective, our self-correcting understanding of justice should not only provide the options for the poor, but also the theoretical and practical foundations for the transformation of unjust social structures.

3. Problems of Theories of Justice

1) Commutative Justice and Distributive Justice

Werpehowski categorizes justice into commutative and distributive justice in the case of general or legal justice.[14] In this section, I mainly discuss arguments and problems related to these two categories in order to construct my understanding of justice. I will particularly point out the limitations of these understandings, and the consequent necessity of an alternative understanding of justice.

Commutative justice: Commutative justice is, according to Bernard V. Brady, concerned with an economic exchange or transaction.[15] Commutative justice also seeks to set moral boundaries that should not be violated by one of the

---

14) William Werpehowski, "Justice," *The Westminster Dictionary of Christian Ethics*, James F. Chiildress and John Macquarrie, ed. (Philadelphia: The Westminster Press, 1986), pp.329-330.

15) Bernard V. Brady, *The Moral Bond of Community* (Washington D.C.: Georgetown Univ. Press, 1998), 109.

parties. In other words, commutative justice prohibits each party from doing any harm to one another in the exchange of the goods by making "equivalence of exchange."[16] Economic decisions to yield the greatest profits should not be constructed so as to harm the involved parties and nor break the moral boundaries in exchange. Harm occurs when one party is in a dominant position in the process of exchange. Thus, the question is how we construct structures that ensure equality in order to achieve commutative justice.[17]

Gunnemann argues that commutative justice is possible under two conditions: Some shared meanings and roughly equal competence of judgment. In his view, "A just exchange can take place only when those exchanging have some shared meanings about what it is that they are exchanging, and some roughly equal competence in judging

---

16) Jon P. Gunnemann, "Capitalism and Commutative Justice," *The Annual of the Society of Christian Ethics* (1985): 103.

17) *Ibid.*

the commodities, their quality, and their value."[18] Problems here include social and religious meanings of the goods that may change, and equal competence in judgment is affected by distortions created by distances.[19] Socio-cultural meanings of the goods can be created, discarded, and recreated with different values. For example, religious and ritual meaning of artifacts from exotic cultures can be discarded in a consumer culture.[20] Moreover, "a world of shared meanings and mutual knowledgeability"[21] is often inhibited by a supplier who manipulates the distances to the market in order to make "extraordinary profits."

Gunnemann suggests alternatives to the problems of

---

18) *Ibid.*

19) The meanings of distance for Gunnemann are not limited to the physical distance. They include different levels of distances such as the degrees of accessibility to information and technology between the supplier and the buyers. For example, the suppliers may limit the accessibility of information on the goods in order to prevent the buyers from making right judgment on the values of the good. *Ibid.*, 104.

20) *Ibid.*, 105.

21) *Ibid.*, 104.

market exchange. Among them are the following: One suggestion is to be suspicious about references to markets that are abstractions from the real world. Real world economies are complex and different from such abstractions. Thus, it is necessary to know specifics about exchanges in order to engage commutative justice. Another is to organize political planning and regulation regarding the exchange of certain commodities in a free market that is always favorable to the stronger party as a solution to economic problems.[22]

From my perspective, commutative justice has some problems. First, the possibilities of injustice are always present in market exchange, because the complex dynamics in society that influence the values of the goods cannot be checked. Moreover, the values and meanings of the goods are often determined by power groups, mostly created by the powers of Western consumerism. For example, the values of the goods can be created and manipulated by advertising and strategies of the suppliers.[23] In this sense, the

---

22) *Ibid.*, 119.

market mechanism is always favorable to the stronger parties not only for the solution to the economic problems, but also for the ongoing creation and development of the economic values and meanings.

Additionally, the premise of a just exchange that requires some shared meanings in market exchange faces the problem that the creation and determination of shared meanings in society are already the results of the unjust asymmetry of the powers present among the parties involved. In fact, when compared to the rich, the poor have fewer opportunities to accessibilities to the process of creating shared meanings and values in market mechanisms. Their opinions and interests are silenced in the process of the determination of shared meanings in society. Thus, commutative justice does not provide a strong ethical basis for the options for the poor.

---

23) For example, the values and social meanings of diamonds are created by the suppliers. Moreover, its supplies are controlled and manipulated by the suppliers.

Second, the terms of the premise for just exchange, "Some roughly equal competence" remains unclear and does not tell us what the meaningful degrees of competence are. The premise may be used as a practical reason to allow the possibility of judgment. Yet, whether the competence remains same in certain circumstances, or, who will define the minimum of one's competence for just exchange, are difficult to answer. Therefore, the premise does not provide a helpful basis to determine the issue of competence between the poor and the rich. Do they have equal power to make shared meanings? Who will judge whose competence? Commutative justice focused on exchange has its own problems to answer.

Distributive justice: Distributive justice is concerned with the community's distribution of social benefits and burdens to individuals and groups.[24] According to Brady, "It reflects on the allocation of social benefits and social burdens to individuals."[25] In distributive justice, the role of the govern-

---

24) Werpehowski,, 330.

ment, social meanings,[26] and the concepts related to of common good are important.

According to Walzer, "The government is morally obligated to distribute public goods fairly to promote the common good."[27] The scarcity of social benefits and the necessity for social obligations require the government to act as a moral agent to distribute benefits and obligations for the organization of society. However, when the government distributes such benefits and obligations, however, the issues of social meanings and "common good" arise.

According to Michael Walzer, "Distributive justice must stand in some relation to the goods that are being distributed"[28] and these goods must stand in some relation to the place and the people to whom they are distributed.[29]

---

25) Brady, 114.

26) Michael Walzer, *Thick and Thin* (Notre Dame: Univ.of Notre Dame Press, 1994), 26.

27) Brady, 114.

28) Walzer, 26.

29) *Ibid.*

Thus, "distributive justice is relative to social meanings."[30] Social meanings change over time and are subject to dispute in discussions of as it relates to distributive justice.

However, it is important to understand that some social meanings of the goods may last long even under serious disputes, and often are protected from the market exchange.[31] Walzer explains, "Indeed, agreements on the most critical social goods are commonly both deep and long lasting, ..."[32] In his view, some shared meanings of the most critical social goods may cross-over cultures.[33] In other words, there are aspects of particularism and universalism in the understanding of social meanings of certain goods. Some shared meanings of the most critical social goods that are

---

30) *Ibid.*

31) In fact, it is a major project of commutative justice to determine what sorts of social goods to be protected from market mechanisms, Gunnemann, 102.

32) Walzer, 28.

33) "This idea of human dignity has broad cross-cultural resonance and intuitive power." Martha C. Nussbaum, *Women and Human Development* (Cambridge: Cambridge Univ. Press, 2000), 72.

generated from local societies and cultures could be shared universally with other local societies and cultures.

The objective of distributive justice is the sharing of common goods, "goods often limited or scarce, that are not wholly 'owned' by any individual but are necessary for human well-being."[34] Brady categorizes four sets of common goods. The first is "fundamental human goods," which include "basic nutrition, security..., and basic freedoms...."[35] They are the basic or necessary conditions for the fulfillment of a human life. Accordingly, the government has the obligation to distribute these goods fairly. The second set refers to public goods or the infrastructure that include "parks, roads, the physical infrastructure of the community, the air, and the water."[36] These goods require "direct action by the government to insure their protection and development."[37] Public goods should be protected from market mechanisms or pri-

---

34) Brady, 114.
35) *Ibid.*, 115.
36) *Ibid.*
37) *Ibid..*

vate individuals because we cannot expect nor can we rely on the fair distribution of these public goods. The third set refers to "communal goods" that include "such elements as social tradition, the modes of communication in a community... the community's history, culture, and language."[38] The means of communication, social traditions, and social narratives are related with the issue of control, and the access to these goods should be fairly or justly distributed. The fourth is "procedural goods" that "contains the practices of the general functions of society, such as law, political participation, and education."[39] These goods should be distributed justly in order for social systems to treat people equally.

The problem related to distributive justice is that we cannot apply distributive justice to some developing countries that do not have resources. Additionally, distributive justice does not provide an effective basis of generating resources.

---

38) *Ibid.*,15-116.
39) *Ibid.*,116.

II. Toward Sustainable Justice 85

On a national level, distributive justice is for a society that at least has a minimum of social resources. Compared to the rich countries whose government should focus on the just distribution of resources, the governments of those poor developing countries are unable to initiate programs for justice in distribution. The poor developing countries often do not have four sets of common goods available to them as suggested by Brady. Some countries cannot provide people with only basic nutrition, security, parks, roads, political participation, and education as common goods. The priority of the government in these countries focuses on the production of such resources, not the distribution of them.

So far, I have discussed two understandings of justice such as commutative justice and distributive justice. In my view, both have specific limitations as described above, though they do provide important aspects related to justice. That is, on the one hand, commutative justice does not provide a strong ethical basis for the options for the poor. On the other hand, distributive justice is inappropriate for some poor countries in which there is a lack of resources. Because the issue of the poor is assumed to be universal, the inapplicability of distributive justice in some cases has its own essential limitation. Therefore, alternative understandings of justice should provide strong ethical basis for the option for the poor, and need to be universal in their application.

2) Justice as Equality and Fairness: John Rawls' Understanding of Justice as Fairness

John Rawls has played an important role in contributing to the development of modern theories of justice.[40] Since his publication of *A Theory of Justice* (1971), he has generated ongoing scholarly debates on justice. Influenced by critical arguments, he recently defended his theory of justice with the publication of *Justice as Fairness: A Restatement.* In the following discussion, I will explain aspects of his theory

---

40) Werpehowski, 331.

in order to point out his limitations and contributions to the developments of contemporary theories of justice. Especially, I will focus on his argument of "the original position."[41]

Rawls explains regarding the original position, "It models what we regard-here and now-as fair conditions under which the representatives of citizens, viewed solely as free and equal persons, are to agree to the fair terms of social cooperation (as expressed by principles of justice) whereby the basic structure is to be regulated."[42] Rawls constructs the possibility of a unanimous agreement among the representatives of citizens in the original position. In that position, the representatives are free and equal, and rational to make the same judgment.

If the free and equal representatives are affected by bargaining advantages, the power of negotiation among the representatives becomes asymmetrical, which results in un-

---

41) John Rawls, "Justice as Fairness: A Restatement," *Justice*, 4th Edition, ed. by James P. Sterba (Belmont: Wadsworth, 2003), 107.

42) *Ibid.*

fair consequences of the discussion. Thus, Rawls tries to solve this problem by limiting the representatives to "the same information about general circumstances of society" with the idea of "the veil of ignorance."[43] He understands that the veil of ignorance is an effective condition by which to remove "differences in bargaining advantages, so that in this and other respects the parties are symmetrically situated." There, his idealization for social agreement is as such: The free and equal representatives of citizens come to the table of political discussion for "primary goods"[44] and cooperate to make the same rational judgment with the veil of ignorance in the original position.

The original position of the representatives is, however, an idealization of specific conditions formulated beyond our real world. Therefore, the representatives, as idealized as free and equal and situated symmetrically without bargaining advantages, are irrelevant to our experiences of the real-

---

43) *Ibid.*, 108.
44) *Ibid.*, 109.

ities in the world. That is, the original position and the veil of ignorance do not reflect the situations of real society. The representatives in the real world are, in fact, directly affected by their own experiences and cultural differences.

In the real world, the representatives are neither fully free and equal, nor fully independent under the influences of our life experiences. In order to construct a realistic theory that does reflect our lives, the differences among the representatives should be fully considered in Rawls' theoretical settings. A valid example of this kind of alternative can be found in Eva Kittay's arguments that address the differences and the needs of care in the case of the dependents and the dependency workers, which are discussed in greater detail in the next section. Thus, the limitations in Rawls's theory require that an alternative theory of justice should be fully attentive to the differences of the moral agents.

4. Elements for fan Alternative Concept of Justice

In the previous sections of this study, I have pointed out the problems and limitations of some theories of justice. Based on my arguments, I have insisted on the necessity for the construction of an alternative understanding of justice. My theoretical concepts of justice that I learn as necessary include the following elements: 1) An alternative understanding of justice should begin with the poor and continue in dialogue with them. 2) Such an understanding should be attentive to the differences of the moral agents, such that the concept of love and care are integral to the understanding. In addition, essential to the understanding should be a focus on the development of the capacities of the moral agent, rather than simply having a focus on the distribution of the resources.

As the issue of the poor is universal, the alternative approach should be universal. A democratic society is an environment in which justice should prevail. Such a society envi-

sions a good society in which mutuality, equality (with attention to the difference), peace, and non-violence prevail.
Finally, an alternative understanding of justice in the good
society oriented towards reconciliation. With these element
in mind, I will try to construct my own understanding of
justice.

1) Difference and Care

Elements of an alternative understanding of justice are
found in Eva F. Kittay's arguments on differences and care.
She challenges the theories of justice that emphasize equality and independence as qualities of a perfect society.[45]
Rawls' theory of justice, for example, supposes that the civil
representatives are free and equal. She argues, however,
that such a supposition disguises the inevitable human conditions of dependence and asymmetries in a life-span, consequently obscure a gender division of labor into the sphere

---

45) Eva Feder Kittay, *Love's Labor* (New York: Routledge, 1999), 4.

of male.[46]

Kittay further argues that equality as an ideal of justice should appreciate "the relational character of difference"[47] and "the values and virtues of care"[48] in order to reflect the realities of the characteristics in our life-spans. Her argument is developed based on the principle of care and the principle of *doulia*. The principle of care insists that, in order to grow, flourish, and survive, each individual requires a caring relationship with significant others who will take a primary responsibility for the person's well-being. The principle of *doulia* argues that we need to provide conditions for others to receive care, as we have required it to survive and thrive. These principles inform us of an approach to distribute social resources to support the relationship of dependency.[49] This approach also provides an ethical norm that suggests that society distributes more social goods to the differences

---

46) *Ibid.*, 14.
47) *Ibid.*, 17.
48) *Ibid.*, 18.
49) *Ibid.*,186.

of needs to care for dependents. In this sense, equality without attending to the differences in dependency relations does not reflect the realities of human life. She argues that if equality is to become a reality reflecting dependency and care, "It must be a *connection-based* equality, and equality that recognizes needs based on our functioning through periods of dependency and caring for dependents. A connection-based equality is one concerned less with resources as such and more with capabilities and functionings."[50] Differences of individuals in dependency relations, necessity of care, and concepts of equality from Kittay's arguments are constructive elements for alternative descriptions of justice that are discussed in the next chapter.

2) Capabilities Approach and Universalism

Martha C. Nussbaum also provides elements that are helpful for constructing concepts of justice. She is con-

---

50) *Ibid.*

cerned with political and economic issues of gender and poverty in the global political economy. She argues, "International political and economic theories should be feminist, attentive... to special problems women face because of sex...."[51]

Nussbaum insists that the governments should provide a basic social minimum to nations,[52] and suggests that a capabilities approach can provide the best ideas to the minimum. The governments are responsible for generating social resources. According to her, the capabilities approach is concerned with "What people are actually able to do and to be-in a way informed by an intuitive idea of a life that is worthy of the dignity of the human being."[53] She tries to make a list of central human capabilities that can be "the object of an *overlapping consensus* among people who otherwise have very different comprehensive conceptions of the

---

51) Nussbaum, 4.
52) *Ibid.*, 5.
53) *Ibid.*,

good."[54] The capabilities should be pursued "for each and every person, treating each as an end and none as a mere tool of the ends of others."[55]

The capabilities approach of Nussbaum focuses on a person's capabilities to do something. It questions the person's inner capabilities, willingness, methods, social positions, and circumstances around the person.[56] Thus, the capabilities approach points out multi-layered political and economic capabilities that the person has and which helps the person to function fully as human beings. However, it does not force the person to follow a prescribed method. Once it addresses and enables socio-political and economic capabilities that the person has, it stops there and leave the choices for them respectfully.[57]

Nussbaum argues that "the capabilities approach is fully universal."[58] She believes that specific elements in many

---

54) *Ibid.*
55) *Ibid.*
56) *Ibid.*, 71.
57) *Ibid.*, 91.

cultures such as narratives and experiences of suffering and poverty, and gender division in society are universal. Some normative ideas, beliefs, and values in diversities of cultures are universal when they are sufficiently attuned.[59] With this idea of universalism, she presents a list of "central human functional capabilities"[60] that could be considered of significant importance cross-culturally.

Where social resources are extremely minimized, theories of commutative justice and distributive justice have limitations as we have studied so far. However, understanding of justice in terms of capabilities approach may fill up the gap of theories. In my perspective, the capabilities approach may provide an ethical basis to claim the governments in the worlds to generate social minimums for nations.

---

58) *Ibid.*, 5.

59) *Ibid.*, 41-59.

60) They are "1. Life, 2. Bodily Health, 3. Bodily Integrity, 4. Senses, Imagination, and Thought, 5. Emotions, 6. Practical Reason, 7. Affiliation, 8. Other Species, 9. Play, 10. Control over One's Environment." *Ibid.*, 78-80.

3) Deliberative Democracy

Iris M. Young offers social environments and means for justice in her arguments. She explains that democratic societies are social environments with the potential that can protect and promote justice.[61] She introduces the deliberative model of democracy that is effectively attentive to the problems of structural injustice. She argues, "The model of deliberative democracy implies a strong meaning of inclusion and political equality which, when implemented, increases the likelihood that democratic decision-making processes will promote justice."[62]

Deliberative democracy has several normative ideals such as "inclusion, equality, reasonableness, and publicity:"[63] Inclusion allows for maximum expression of opinions; Political equality promotes "free and equal opportunity to

---

61) Iris M. Young, *Inclusion and Democracy* (Oxford: Oxford Univ. Press, 2000), 5.

62) *Ibid.*, 5.

63) *Ibid.*, 23.

speak;" Reasonableness refers to the participants' disposition to listen to others with respect and an open mind; Publicity requires participants to be accountable to one another.[64]

In the process of interactions with these ideals, deliberative democracy invites participants into the decision-making process and allows them free and equal opportunity to express their opinions. The participants in turn are reasonable and open-minded in the process of discussion. Also, they are accountable to others in their motivation to win their consent, appealing to a common good.

In Young's ideas of the deliberative model, democracy is the best and the only effective means with which to protect and promote the interests of citizens, to check the abusive political powers, to change institutions, and to solve problems and conflicts collectively in the process of open discussion and with respect. Therefore, although there may be possibilities for the reinforcement of the structural inequal-

---

64) *Ibid.*, 23-25.

ities of wealth and power in the democratic procedures, and of manipulation of the procedure by the privileged to marginalize the voices and issue of the less privileged,[65] she prefers attempting to achieving more just conditions within democratic institutions than to achieving them outside the democratic means by way of authoritarian or revolutionary forces.[66] She believes that the attempt to achieve justice outside of the democracy may not be always wrong; yet, it is more risky in terms of producing further injustice.[67] She argues, "Organizing and political mobilization within formally democratic institutions and norms is usually the only realistic option for oppressed and disadvantaged people and their allies to improve social relations and institutions."[68]

Young provides a strong political theory for the participant environments and procedural means for justice. She believes that deliberative democracy is one of the best politi-

---

65) *Ibid.*, 34.
66) *Ibid.*, 35.
67) *Ibid.*
68) *Ibid.*

cal forms to promote justice for the oppressed and the marginalized, because, in her ideas, democratic society has inner
powers for the correction of social problems. With a vision
for progress, she believes that structural injustice in a democratic society can change in support of greater justice
through the deliberative democratic processes.

4) Reconciliation

John W. De Gruchy understands reconciliation as restora-t
ive justice.[69] He justifies that understanding reconciliation
should expand from theological expression to social and
political expressions. For him, reconciliation is not only an
aspect of theological process, but also includes need for so-c
ial engagement and consequent political transformation. He
insists that reconciliation is "a human and social process that
requires theological explanation, and a theological con-cept

---

69) John W. De Gruchy, *Reconciliation* (Minneapolis: Fortress Press,
2002), 2.

seeking human and social embodiment."[70] He believes that reconciliation is "an action, praxis and movement before it be comes a theory or dogma" as well as "a process in which we become engaged at the heart of the struggle for justice and peace in the world."[71] For De Gruchy, reconciliation as rest orative justice is a major goal of society.

In the theological sphere, the Christian message of the Gospel, God's saving activity in the world, narratives of re-demption, place reconciliation at the center of the messages. De Gruchy insists that the Church should be "the agent of reconciliation, representing its embodiment in history.[72] He understands the Church as "the vicarious representative of the new humanity,"[73]which means, otherwise, "a sacra-mental community."[74] He argues, "The sacraments rightly understood and practiced within the worship life of the

---

70) *Ibid.*, 20.
71) *Ibid.*, 21.
72) *Ibid.*, 5.
73) *Ibid.*, 94.
74) *Ibdi.*, 95.

Church play a central role in shaping Christian community and its witness to God's reconciliation (96)."

In the social and political spheres, reconciliation is represented in more sophisticated forms. According to De Gruchy, in the process of seeking reconciliation in South Africa, TRC (Truth and Reconciliation Committee) set the goal to foster national reconciliation[75] as means of the healing of society. Reconciliation was pursued by "creating space for interfacing"[76] and by telling the truth. However, there was a paradox during the process. That is, "The single-minded pursuit of justice can lead to destructive vengeance, just as the pursuit of reconciliation without justice perpetuates evil."[77] He finds answers to the paradox through the experiences in the further process of reconciliation. He claims, "What is truly remarkable in the struggle for justice, however, is not the sound of fury, but the word of forgive-

---

75) *Ibid,.* 147.
76) *Ibid.,* 148.
77) *Ibid.,* 169.

ness, a key moment in the process of reconciliation. Yet it is only when we listen to the outrage of victims that we can begin to appreciate their offer of forgiveness."[78]

Finally, De Gruchy combines theological expression with social and political spheres. He argues that "restorative justice has to do with renewing God's covenant and therefore the establishing of just power relations without which reconciliation remains elusive."[79] He continues that restorative justice seeks to bind separated people together "in mutual care and responsibility for each other and for the larger society."[80] However, we find gaps between contemporary political realities and Christian eschatology. According to him, the gaps between historical realities and eschatological visions will be bridged by hope of fulfillment of reconciliation and healing in covenantal relationship of God with people.

---

78) *Ibid.*, 170.
79) *Ibid.*, 204.
80) *Ibid.*

De Gruchy illustrated reconciliation in terms of restorative justice. According to him, reconciliation is the ultimate goal of society that Christians should pursue in the hope of realization. De Gruchy helps us to understand justice as an active source of power in the process of healing of broken relations in society. In his ideas, reconciliation recognizes individual and structural evil that has been perpetuated in society, and effectively acts to bring about healing in forgiveness.[81]

5. Descriptions of Justice

1) Some Clarifications and Concepts

Before attempting to construct my own concept of justice based on the previous discussions, certain clarifications need to be made. My concepts of justice are descriptive and

---

81) *Ibid.*, 178.

synthetically constructed based on the following elements; a) Difference and Care; b) the Capabilities Approach; c) Deliberative Democracy; d) Reconciliation; and e) Sustainability. Because my understanding of justice functions critically and complements the theories of justice previously discussed, it can be considered a model of *alternative* justice.

In order to help with this clarification, it is useful to label my own concept of justice as a form of *sustainable justice,* or, a justice model of *living and growing together with the vulnerable.* I am aware that the use of the modifiers, *sustainable,* and *of living and growing,* may restrict descriptions of justice. That is, the term, sustainable, has been used in the discourse of the environmental justice. However, my intention for using such terms is for purposes of clarification. I do not insist that my concept of justice and the use of such terms are definitive. Rather, my concept of justice is flexible, as I understand it in terms of process. Thus, it is my claim that my intention for using these modifiers is simply to clarify the aspects of my own concept of justice.

Moreover, I use the meaning of the term, sustainable, as it is defined in Webster's II New College dictionary: 1) To keep in existence: maintain; 2) To provide with nourishment or sustenance; 3) To support from below; 4) To support the spirits, vitality, or resolution of: encourage; 5) Endure or withstand: bear up; 6) To experience or suffer (loss or injury); 7) To affirm the validity or justice of; 8) To corroborate: confirm.[82]

According to these definitions, sustainable justice, thus, can be understood as justice that is able to keep the lives of human beings (especially the poor, the marginalized, and the oppressed) in existence (instead of letting them die); to provide human beings with nourishment, to support them from below, to support their spirits, vitality, to suffer with them, and to endure their illnesses and frailties. Meanwhile, using the words, *living together,* highlights the need for the

---

82) *Wester's II New College Dictionary* (Boston: Houghton Mifflin Company, 1999).

solidarity with the vulnerable and the perishable.[83)]
Growing together emphasizes the process of the fulfillment
of one's life to the full extension of life. The use of sustainable justice, or, the justice of living and growing together,
emphasizes the importance of *life* in a sense that Nussbaum
argues, that is, as the first central capabilities, "Being able to
live to the end of a human life of normal length; not dying
prematurely, or before one's life is so reduced as to be not
worth living."[84)]

2) Descriptions of My Own Concept of Justice

My own concept of justice, as sustainable justice, or, the
justice of living and growing together with the vulnerable,
does, therefore, include explanations regarding the starting
point, the methods, and the goals of justice. Because I have

---

83) Young, 222-224.

84) Martha C. Nussbaum, *Women and Human Development* (Cam-
    bridge: Cambridge University Press, 2000), 78.

previously discussed these ideas and elements of justice, it may seem redundant to speak of them again. However, my arguments here may be viewed as the refinements of the interaction between those ideas and justice, and of their usefulness in understanding of justice.

First, the starting point of justice is, in fact, the concrete situation of the poor and the struggle of the option for the poor. In contemporary society, people live in complex social, political, and economic relations. In our normal conditions, we can neither escape from these complex relations, nor can we live outside of the web of these relations. However, people tend to think abstractly and to separate themselves from these relations under the influences of market mechanisms. From my perspective, an individual in market systems reflects the most influential results from these abstractions. The most basic forms of free market systems understand people as free, equal, and rational beings who preclude emotions and interdependency in order to make the sum of each individual's economic activities the mechanically balanced results of society.

In my ideas, part of the problem of contemporary society lies in the dynamics generated in market systems. For example, the rich and the privileged are able to distance themselves from the poor, psychologically and physically, and to marginalize and oppress the poor and powerless in the dynamics of abstraction. De Gruchy's emphasis on "meeting face-to-face and entering into a conversation"[85] as a condition for reconciliation validate my argument here. Facing the tendencies of abstraction and separation in our society, justice should highlight the inter-connectedness in our social relations.

In my beliefs, if justice is understood as sustainable justice, it can provide a clearer justification for the arguments of inter-connectedness and interdependency. Because sustainable justice argues that it is just to live and grow together, it provides an ethical basis to care and responsibility for others. Especially, the poor represent the starting point be-

---

85) De Gruchy, 151.

cause, in order to grow together, they need more care than the rich, in general. The options for the poor are better justified in the ideas of sustainable justice, because sustainable justice essentially implies the idea of solidarity: That is, we are living together and should live together. Thus, sustainable justice emphasizes solidarity with the poor, and asks our compassion and conversion regarding options for the poor.

Second, justice pursues equality, and this equality should reflect the realities of human life such as differences and interdependency among people, acknowledging their respective needs and care. Just society must realize the differences of each member and their respective needs, and the responsibility to respond to them accordingly. As Kittay understands the ideal of justice as equality[86] and tries to refine its changed meaning in society, including the task of care into a just society will not be simply a mathematical addition of a virtue to many, but rather a change of relational respon-

---

86) Kittay, 18.

sibility and the appropriate responses of society. Therefore, a just society should understand and respond to the preference of giving care to the poor in a relationship of interdependency as exercise of equality. In addition, a just society should create reciprocal environments of giving and receiving care to each other as Kittay argues.[87]

For example, distributive justice is concerned with social goods and the way they are distributed. In the effort to achieve consensus regarding the meaning of social goods, a just society with these ideas of equality in differences and care should respond to the voices of the poor who have often been marginalized and silenced in contemporary society. Moreover, it should include more voices from the poor because they have been systematically marginalized.

Following this process, I argue that market mechanisms should not be the only means by which to control accessibility to the scarcity of goods, including common goods. I believe that our agreements from this idea of a just society

---

87) *Ibid.*, 186-187.

that includes the virtue of care and responsibility into the accessibility may check the omnipotence of market mechanism. Ideas of sustainable justice that justify *living and growing together* may help the redistribution of social goods in its innate appeal being in solidarity with the poor.

In the case of the developing countries experiencing poverty, sustainable justice with the capabilities approach will generate governmental programs that provide resources needed for the "central human functional capabilities" of their people. No discrimination on any basis whatsoever can be justified in a capabilities approach. In a gendered society, especially in the poor developing countries, women are not equally treated as men because of their gender, and are consequently more vulnerable than men. Therefore, sustainable justice, combined with the capabilities approach should respond to the needs of the poor women. For example, in the process of social consensus, the voices of the poorest women should be considered more seriously, and accessibilities to social goods should be more open to women who are more vulnerable than men. Moreover, in my belief, the government's programs should have a preference geared toward the realization of the central human capabilities of the poorest women in developing countries because they are among the most vulnerable. Thus, I believe that the realization of physical health of the poor women should have priority to that of the poor men because of their significant vulnerability.

Third, justice, as the virtue and the goal of society, is best promoted in democratic society through the deliberative democratic processes. In our society, justice is one of the cardinal virtues.[88] We value justice and often try to project it as a norm of society. As a value and a goal of society, justice must be understood as a continuous process for the development of a "good" society.

According to Young, deliberative democracy provides the best and the most effective tools and environments. Young believes that deliberative democracy would be able

---

88) Brady, 124.

to include and invite the poor to the table of discussions in order to listen to their voices with open-minds. She believes that democracy promotes justice through the democratic means of the decision-making process.[89]

Therefore, justice is understood as a process, and, as such, is achieved through continuous dialogue with the poor in democratic societies. As a process, justice also requires interaction with ideas, values, and people. The meanings and the achievements of justice thus lie in the deliberate process of open discussions and mutual consensus among self-critical participants of society. In other words, justice is facilitated through democratic means in deliberate democratic environments that include and prioritize the voices of the poor in solidarity with them.

My understanding of justice as *living and growing together with the vulnerable*, also reflects the aspects of process, in itself. On the one hand, it supposes a process of an organic growth in the words of *living and growing* that value the ful-

---

89) Young, 223.

fillment of life. On the other hand, in the term, *together,* it supposes that other members are dealt with care and respect. With the term, *together,* my understanding of justice claims that the poor who had been marginalized should not be neglected any longer, but need to be respected as equal members together. I believe that my understanding of justice, as *living and growing together with the vulnerable,* can be an effective concept of justice as the process in democratic environments.

Finally, the ultimate goal of justice is reconciliation. According to De Gruchy, the goal of justice is not vengeance but reconciliation. It is not death but life. Reconciliation, as restorative justice, focuses on healing. In the process of achieving the goal of forgiveness, restorative justice can heal the broken relationships caused by individuals and structural injustices, and can stop the perpetuations of the cycle of violence.[90]

In what ways can sustainable justice speak of reconcilia-

---

90) De Gruchy, 172.

tion as the ultimate goal of justice? Can reconciliation be the ultimate goal of sustainable justice, as well? In other words, is it valid for us to understand reconciliation through the concept of sustainable justice? With modifiers, broad meanings of justice have been both restricted and refined as sustainable justice. My concept of sustainable justice centralizes *life* that should flourish to its fullest extent of life in meaningful relationship with all others. As reconciliation as restorative justice emphasizes the importance of life in the process of forgiveness and healing, it has a shared ground to work with my understanding of sustainable justice.

Further, sustainable justice makes a universal claim that the intrinsic human needs and capabilities should be valued and fulfilled preferably for the urgent need of the most vulnerable, in order for all of us to flourish through the full extension of our lives in meaningful social relations with each other in communities. Thus, sustainable justice prefers options for the poor, because they are the least well-off and the most vulnerable due to the injustices of our social systems.

In the process of achieving justice toward reconciliation, we can realize the potential to continuously participate in the struggle of the poor with solidarity.

6. Conclusion: Toward Sustainable Justice

In my essay, I have attempted to provide descriptions of justice using my own terms. In order to do so, I have studied specific theories of justice and pointed out their limitations from my perspectives. My criticisms of the theories have focused on their concepts of equality and understandings of the moral agents. Most of the criticism as well as constructions of my own concept of justice are indebted to theories of differences and care, the capabilities approach, deliberative democracy, and reconciliation.

As for my own concept of justice, I have used the term, *sustainable justice, or, justice of living and growing together with the vulnerable*. It is based on my beliefs of usefulness that I have tried to explain my own understanding of justice. Despite their limitations, I have deliberately attempted to describe my concept of justice through the terms, sustainable justice, and further, through the justice of living and growing together with the vulnerable. In my beliefs, the use of these terms is valid because of their emphasis on *life* and because of their respective potential to highlight the concepts of process, care, and responsibility, as well as interdependency with each other.

In my understandings, justice starts from the reality of the poor and prefers options for the poor. Justice pursues equality with attention to difference and care. Justice, as the value and the goal of society, is best promoted in the process of the deliberative democracy. Justice is concerned with the distribution and exchange of social resources, however, where these resources are limited, human capabilities and social minimums should be created by the governments. Justice seeks restoration, not violent vengeance.

I believe that these descriptions of justice above are better understood when used with the modified terms, sustainable justice, or, the justice of living and growing together with the vulnerable. Then, in such beliefs, a question may arise. "Could this understanding of sustainable justice be realized in our society?" My answers are resonant with that of De Gruchy: "Hope enables us to believe that we can achieve some meaningful expression of justice, reconciliation and healing here and now even though the ultimate goal must always remain beyond our grasp."[91]

---

91) *Ibid.*, 212.

Bibliography

Brady, Bernard V.. *The Moral Bond of Community*. Washington D.C.: Georgetown Univ. Press, 1998.

De Gruchy, John W.. *Reconciliation*. Minneapolis: Fortress Press, 2002.

Gunnemann, Jon P.. "Capitalism and Commutative Justice." in *The Annual of the Society of Christian Ethics*, 1985.

Kittay, Eva Feder. *Love's Labor*. New York: Routledge, 1999.

Nussbaum, Martha C.. *Women and Human Development*. Cambridge: Cambridge Univ. Press, 2000.

O'Brien, John. *Theology and the Option for the Poor*. The Liturgical Press: Collegeville, 1992.

Rawls, John. "Justice as Fairness: A Restatement." *Justice,* 4th Edition, ed. by James P. Sterba. Belmont: Wadsworth, 2003.

Wallis, Jim. *The Soul of Politics*. New York: A Harvest Book, 1995.

Walzer, Michael. *Thick and Thin*. Notre Dame: Univ. of Notre Dame Press, 1994.

Werpehowski, William. "Justice." *The Westminster Dictionary of Christian Ethics*. James F. Childress and John Macquarrie, ed. Philadelphia: The Westminster Press, 1986.

Young, Iris M.. *Inclusion and Democracy*. Oxford: Oxford Univ. Press, 2000.

Wester's II New College Dictionar. Boston: Houghton Mifflin Company, 1999.

III

Heinz Kohut and Narcissism*

1. Developments in Understanding Narcissism

Because of the ambiguity of the term, narcissism, as pointed out previously, it is necessary to trace and define the meaning of narcissism. The term, narcissism, originates in the Greek myth of Narcissus, who had a stubborn pride as a result of his beauty and consequently destroyed himself

---

* This essay is a part of my Ph. D. dissertation. Yong Sup Song, *A Christian Ethics of Empathy for Communities of Faith in the Midst of Racial Conflicts: Violence, Racism, and Narcissism in the Los Angeles Uprising of 1992* (Madison, NJ: Drew University, 2012).

due to love for his own reflection that clearly appeared in a spring. Havelock Ellis, a British physician and psychologist, used this myth to describe the psychological state of male autoeroticism in his article, "Auto-erotism" in 1898, using the term, "narcissus-like".[1] One year later, Paul Näcke in 1899, using the term, "narcismus," noted that narcissism, as a sexual perversion, denotes "the attitude of a person who treats his own body in the same way in which the body of a sexual object is ordinarily treated...."[2] Later, Isidor I. Sadger, an Austrian physician and psychoanalyst, used narcissism in discussing psychoanalytic ideas in a paper in 1908, which was referred to by Wilhelm Stekel in 1908.[3]

In 1910, Freud first used the term, "Narcismus," that is, "narcissistic," in his essay in a footnote to "Three Essay on the

---

1) Havelock Ellis, "Auto-erotism: A psychological study," *Alienist and Neurologist,* Vol.19 (1898): 260-299. Refer to Chessick, 4.

2) Sigmund Freud, "On Narcissism: An Introduction," 17.

3) Sydney E. Pulver, "Narcissism: The Term and the Concept," ed. Andrew P. Morrison, M.D., *Essential Papers on Narcissism* (New York: New York University Press, 1986), 93.

Theory of Sexuality (1905)."[4] In this essay, he described narcissism "as a phase in the libidinal development of inverts. Narcissism here still referred to a specific perversion."[5] Freud distinguished narcissism as a primary and a secondary narcissism in his writing, "On Narcissism: An Introduction," in 1914. According to Freud, a primary narcissism is a normal narcissism that is "the libidinal complement to the egoism of the instinct of self-preservation, a measure of which may justifiably be attributed to every living creature."[6] He argued that a secondary narcissism is a pathological occurrence when the primary narcissism does not develop into object love, so that a secondary narcissism "has the significance of a perversion that has absorbed the whole of the subject's sexual life...."[7]

---

4) Chessic, 4.

5) Pulver, 93.

6) Sigmund Freud, "On Narcissism: An Introduction," ed. Andrew P. Morrison, *Essential Papers on Narcissism* (New York: New York University Press, 1986), 18.

7) *Ibid.*, 17.

Sydney Pulver, a psychiatrist, explains further, "Freud describes a primary narcissism in terms of an initial libidinal investment of psychic energy in the (predifferentiated) ego – a state of symbiotic bliss, which inevitably becomes altered with separation/individuation, as libidinal cathexis shifts from the ego to objects.... Secondary narcissism refers to a condition in which libido is withdrawn from external objects and turned anew onto the ego, or cathected to objects internalized within the ego."[8] Under the influence of Freud, narcissism is generally defined as "a concentration of psychological interest upon the self"[9] in classical perspectives.

However, Kohut suggested a different understanding of narcissism, although he maintained continuity between Freudian ego psychology and his own self psychology in his early writings.[10]

---

8) Morrison, 13.
9) Pulver, 107.
10) Chessic, 6.

Narcissism, within my general outlook, is defined not by the target of the instinctual investment (i.e. whether it is the subject himself or other people) but by the nature of quality of the instinctual charge. The child, for example, invests other people with narcissistic cathexes and thus experiences them narcissistically, i.e. as self-object. The expected control over such (self-object) others is then closer to the concept of the control which a grownup expects to have over his own body and mind than to the concept of the control which he expects to have over others.[11)]

In this argument, Kohut suggested his own definition of narcissism that is different from that of Freud, using Freud's terms. Allen Siegel, a psychiatrist and psychoanalysis, clarifies Kohut's arguments as follows: "He [Kohut] asserts that narcissism has its own developmental line, with unique configurations and developmental endpoints, and differs with Freud's concept of object love as the endpoint in the matura-

---

11) Heinz Kohut, *The Analysis of the Self,* 26-27. For Kohut's similar arguments, see also, 32-33.

tion of narcissism."[12]

Several scholars have further explained and evaluated the distinctiveness of Kohut's ideas of narcissism. According to Siegel, Kohut "understands narcissism as a normal part of life, present from birth to death, not to be relinquished in favor of object love. For Kohut, narcissism has a natural course of development that eventuates in a whole and functioning self,"[13] and thus, as a normal and natural part of life. Leonard M. Hummel, in his article, remarked further, "Narcissism could be both necessary and helpful. Though we may express our narcissistic needs in immature ways, we are nevertheless constituted by them to attach to others whom we admire, to others who admire us, and also to others with whom we experience a sense of kinship."[14]

---

12) Allen M. Siegel, *Heinz Kohut and the Psychology of the Self* (New York, NY: Routledge, 1996), 59.

13) *Ibid.*, 118.

14) Leonard M. Hummel, "Heinz Kohut and Empathy: A Perspective from a Theology of the Cross," *Word & World*, Volume XXI, No. 1 (2001): 66.

Narcissism as a natural course of development of the self is now understood positively, as being necessary in development, a position that is different from Freud who understood it negatively such as a perversion, or, pathology.

Consistent with other scholars, Ivan J. Miller explains, "Kohut (1971, 1977, 1984) presents the idea that a narcissistic line of development – parallel to the development of the drives – is necessary to the development of a healthy and cohesive self."[15] Siegel further evaluates the uniqueness of Kohut's ideas, stating "Kohut's idea is momentous, for it suggests that narcissism is neither obnoxious nor pathological."[16]

According to Charles B. Strozier's evaluation of Kohut's narcissism, what is an important idea in Kohut is his concern "with the quality of the way we relate to others, rather than the mere fact of otherness"[17] in Kohut's discussion about

---

15) Ivan J. Miller, "Interpersonal Vulnerability and Narcissism: A Conceptual Continuum for Understanding and Treating Narcissistic Psychopathology," *Psychotherapy: Theory, Research, Practice, Training*, Vol. 29, Issue 2 (1992): 216.

16) Siegel, 59.

narcissism as a "quality of instinctual charge."[18] As the infant attempts to have control over others experiencing them as selfobject, the adults also experience others as part of the self, even when they are grown up, if the **self structure** is underdeveloped psychologically. Strozier explains, "Others (and their symbolic equivalents) are used to form the fabric of our beings and at the same time are experienced as part of the self. These are the 'self-object.'"[19] Kohut believed that the underdeveloped self could be strengthened and become cohesive "primarily by developing selfobject relationships."[20]

Therefore, the distinctiveness of Kohut's understanding of narcissism that is different from Freud may be summarized as follows: Kohut understands that narcissism has its own developmental line. In addition, Kohut focuses on the

---

17) Charles B. Strozier, *Heinz Kohut: The Making of Psychoanalyst* (New York: Other Press, 2001), 195. Charles Strozier is a professor of history at John Jay college and the Graduate Center, CUNY as well as a psychoanalyst.

18) *Ibid.*, 194.

19) *Ibid.*, 195.

20) Miller, 217.

quality of our way of making relationship with others. For Kohut, narcissism is defined as the underdeveloped structure of the self that experiences others as part of the self. As a primary narcissism, at the stage of early infancy, the self experiences the parents as the selfobject and the self structure is being developed by the quality experience with the selfobject toward either object love or mature narcissism. However, when the self experiences chronic traumas in its life time, the self structure does not develop fully and remain in its immature status.

2. Kohut's Psychology of the Self: Aspects of Narcissism

Before Kohut, the most popular explanation of the self was probably that of George H. Mead,[21] who understood

---

21) George Herbert Mead was a American philosopher, sociologist, and social psychologist famous in the development with

the *self* "as arising out of social interaction and having no innate separate existence,"[22] while a *person* was understood as a being "driven primarily by instinctual desires to attach to other persons in order to gratify those desires."[23] Unlike such popular definition of the self, however, Kohut defined the self in terms of psychology "as a cohesive configuration, experienced as a sense of self with a feeling of wholeness and well being."[24]

In his writing about the self, Kohut used many terms in order to represent his ideas that include "cohesive self," "nuclear self" and "bipolar self." However, according to Phill Mollon,[25] "Kohut seems not to have clearly differentiated between his use of the terms 'cohesive self', 'nuclear self'

---

pragmatism who worked with John Dewey.

22) Chessic, 81.

23) Leonard M. Hummel, "Heinz Kohut and Empathy: A Perspective from a Theology of the Cross," *Word & World*, Volume XXI, No. 1 (2001): 66.

24) Chessic, 84.

25) Phill Mollon, Ph.D., is a psychoanalyst and member of the Independent Group of the British Psycho-Analytical Society.

and 'bipolar self'. From Mollon's perspective, these terms all appear to have similar meanings."[26] Therefore, it may be confusing to differentiate the meaning of these similar terms in different contexts in his publications.

In my understanding, Kohut uses these terms in order to explain core qualities centralized in *the* self. In other words, these terms seem to point out some different nuances of the same core self, though they may have similar meanings. For example, the term, "cohesive self," represents the oneness and wholeness of the self as the status and goal in the self throughout one's life, while "nuclear self" points out the core and centrality of the self out of the possible many selves in a person. Finally, the "bipolar self" represents the structure of the nuclear self. His use of "bipolar self" may help one to understand the bipolarity and dissimilarity of two poles residing in the nuclear self, though he used the terms, "nuclear self" and "bipolar self," more frequently than "cohesive self."

---

26) Phil Mollon, *Releasing the Self: The Healing Legacy of Heinz Kohut* (London: Whurr, 2001), 34.

Initially, Kohut grounded his theory within the spectrum of Freud and (re)interpreted the psychological concepts of Freud. However, he learned that Freudian drive psychology had empirical problems in dealing with narcissistic patients whose psyches could be positioned in-between neurosis and borderline conditions. In Kohut's practice, the Freudian drive psychology was found to be undesirable for treating patients in clinical settings. While Freud's method mainly sought the knowledge of the psychological aspects of the narcissistic patients, assuming it to be an incurable psychological status, Kohut began to realize that patients suffering from narcissism could be suffering from such presupposition and knowledge stemmed from traditional Freudian psychology. Based on his clinical experiences with the narcissistic patients, Kohut argued in support of the necessity of a new approach to deal with patients of narcissism. Kohut believed that if a proper analysis with deep attention to the patients' relationship with selfobject is performed, narcissistic patients who show narcissistic transference to a psychoanalyst[27] may restore the undeveloped structure of the self by the methods of empathy, mirroring, idealizing, and optimal frustration in proper relationship with selfobject.

Therefore, Kohut's psychology of the self has distinctive characteristics compared to Freud's psychopathological approach on narcissism. On the one hand, Freud believed in the single developmental line of narcissism maturing into object love with a negative attitude toward its curability. In his psychological analysis of the patients, he sought the knowledge of the unconscious area of the ego of patients confronting their resistance as a necessary method, focusing on the direction of the sexual investment of libido onto the ego. On the other hand, Kohut believed in the two developmental lines of object love and narcissism that were di-

---

27) Kohut argues in *The Analysis of the Self*, "The relative stability of this narcissistic transference amalgamation, however, is the prerequisite for the performance of the analytic task (the systematic process of working through) in the pathogenic narcissistic areas of the personality," 32.

rected to either object love or mature narcissism respectively with a positive attitude toward its curability. In his clinical settings for the analysis, he sought for an understanding of the nuclear self of the patients, accepting their resistance as a natural process for survival and maturity, while focusing on the quality of the relationship of the nuclear self with its selfobject.

Because Kohut's approach is not only insightful but also challenging to Freudian drive psychology that has been a traditional approach among his contemporary, Kohut developed his ideas cautiously and gradually from the traditional psychology. Probably, because of his caution and intention to remain in the tradition at least to some degree, Kohut' arguments in his writings were complicated in style and difficult to read.[28] Thus, some important concepts of Kohut's psychology are better to be read chronologically, in order to facilitate the understanding of his ideas. By understanding his key concepts, one can find usefulness for the applic-

---

28) Siegel, 194-196.

ability of his concepts into the situations of social conflict such as the L.A. riots in 1992.

From his early writings beginning in 1948,[29] Kohut demonstrated his interests in narcissism strongly based on Freud. Even when Kohut developed his ideas on narcissism and suggested a necessity of a new approach to narcissistic disorder in the 1960s, he did not completely dissociate himself from Freud.[30] In his major writings on narcissism, such as "Formation and Transformation of Narcissism" in 1966 and *The Analysis of the Self* in 1971, Kohut illustrates his association with Freud despite the uniqueness of his theory and gradual development of his own ideas within his publications.

In his "Formation and Transformation of Narcissism," Kohut explains the narcissistic self and the idealized parent imago in relation to Freud's concepts of *id, ego, and*

---

29) Kohut's first article, "Death in Venice by Thomas Mann: A Story About the Disintegration of Artistic Sublimation" was written in 1948, however, it was published after Mann's death in 1957.
30) Siegel, 3.

superego. In this article, Kohut explains that the narcissistic self is similar to the "purified pleasure ego" in Freud's term, "a stage in development in which everything pleasant, good, and perfect is considered as part of a rudimentary self..." as a prestage of the narcissistic self.[31] On the other hand, the idealized parent imago is the counter part of the narcissistic self, which is later called as the grandiose self. Kohut explains the idealized parent imago as follows, "Idealization may of course be properly described as an aspect of narcissism, i.e., of the (still undifferentiated) original bliss, power, perfection, and goodness which is projected on the parent figure during a phase when these qualities become gradually separated into perfection pertaining to pleasure, or power, or knowledge, or beauty, or morality."[32]

One of Kohut's major publications, *Analysis of the Self*, published in 1971 still refers to this stance under the influence of Freud. For example, while Kohut argues for the con-

---

31) Kohut, "Forms and Transforms of Narcissism," 63-64.
32) *Ibid.*, 64.

cept of the self as "a structure within the mind since (a) it is cathected with instinctual energy and (b) it has continuity in time, i.e., it is enduring,"[33] he explains it in comparison with the Freudian concepts of *id, ego, superego.* This study demonstrates Kohut's ideas on narcissism as he substitutes the term, "the narcissistic self" with "the grandiose self."[34] In this book, Kohut explains the preference to the grandiose self, while the concept of the idealization remains unchanged. Kohut defines the term, *grandiose,* as follows:

> The terms 'grandiose' and 'exhibitionistic' refer to a broad spectrum of phenomena, ranging from the child's solipsistic world view and his undisguised pleasure in being admired, and from the gross delusions of the paranoiac and the crudely sexual acts of the adult pervert, to aspects of the mildest, most aim-inhibited, and nonerotic satisfaction of adults with themselves, their functioning, and their achievements.[35]

---

33) Kohut, *The Analysis of the Self,* xv.
34) *Ibid.,* 26.

For Kohut, the term *grandiose self* was used from the publication of the analysis of the self, instead of the previously
used term, *narcissistic self,* "to designate the grandiose and
exhibitionistic structure which is the counterpart of the *idealized parent imago.*"

According to Kohut, both "the grandiose self" and "the
idealized parent imago" are a result of the disturbance of
"the equilibrium of primary narcissism."[36] The disturbance
of the equilibrium of primary narcissism in the infant that results from the limitation of maternal care is unavoidable.[37]
What is important is that the child has a psychological mechanism to replace the original bliss by establishing the grandiose self and the idealized parent imago within manageable
frustration experiences.[38] It is a psychological survival
mechanism for the child to build and maintain the cohesive-

---

35) Kohut, *The Analysis of the Self,* 25-26; Kohut, "Forms and
   Transformations of Narcissism," 64.
36) Kohut, *The Analysis of the Self,* 25.
37) *Ibid.*
38) *Ibid.*

ness of the self in understanding and living around the world that is not perfect or pleasant for it.

According to Kohut, these two structures coexist and their developmental lines are largely independent.[39] Furthermore, the qualities of these two structures are formed by frustration to the degree that the child takes into the self. Kohut argues, "Under optimal developmental conditions, the exhibitionism and grandiosity of the archaic grandiose self are gradually tame, and the whole structure ultimately becomes integrated into the adult personality and supplies the instinctual fuel for our ego-synchronic ambitions and purposes, for the enjoyment of our activities, and for important aspect of our self-esteem."[40] However, if the child experiences narcissistic traumas, narcissistic needs of the grandiose self are retained in the self. Kohut explains, "If the child, however, suffers severe narcissistic traumas, then the grandiose self does not merge into the relevant ego content

---

39) *Ibid.*,27.
40) Kohut, *The Analysis of the Self,* 27-28.

but is retained in its unaltered form and strives for the fulfillment of its archaic aims."[41] The **self structure** of the child is fragmented, unhealthy, and not cohesive. Thus, even when the child grows up, as an adult, he/she strives to build the fragmented structure of the self by absorbing other people as part of the psychic structure of the self.

In his later major work, *The Restoration of the Self,* published in 1977, Kohut attempted to break off the links of his psychology from the psychology of the drive, by boldly arguing, "The primary psychological configurations in the child's experiential world are not drives...."[42] In his text, he also expanded his earlier ideas in the concept of "the Bipolar Self"[43] as well as other ideas in detail. However, some traits of his departure from Freud may be found in his essays written in 1974, "Remarks About the Formation of the Self." In

---

41) *Ibid.,* 28.

42) Kohut, *The Restoration of the Self,* 171.

43) Siegel explains, "Kohut made his break with what he calls the classical 'mental apparatus' psychology in *The Restoration of the Self* (1977)...." Siegel, 105.

this essay, for example, Kohut suggested a "two-line development" that is "Y"-shaped starting from "autoerotism" (experience of parts and part functions) via "archaic narcissism"(nuclear self) and developing either toward "object love" or toward "mature narcissism"(mature self-esteem and transformation of narcissism),[44] instead of explaining the self psychology from the Freudian perspectives in a "single-line development from autoerotism via narcissism to object love."[45]

In other words, Kohut found that there is a second line of development that leads to mature narcissism instead of object love. Furthermore, in Kohut's argument of the second

---

44) Kohut, "Remarks About the Formation of the Self," In *The Search for the Self: Selected Writings of Heinz Kohut: 1950-1978.* Vol. 2., Heinz Kohut, ed. Paul H. Ornstein (New York: International Universities Press, 1978), 764-765. Please refer to figure 5 and 6 for this explanation.

45) Kohut, "Remarks About the Formation of the Self," May, 1974, presented at the Wednesday Research Seminar of the Chicago Institute for Psychoanalysis in January, 1975, Kohut, *The Search for the Self,* Vol. 2., 764.

line of development, he claimed two sub-categories within this second axis toward mature narcissism (mature self) in the nuclear self. Ornstein explains Kohut's ideas further that, in the developmental line toward mature narcissism, there is a "second axis in which two separate lines of development lead from *autoerotism to narcissism to higher forms of narcissism*. He [Kohut] specified the existence of these two parallel developmental lines as the grandiose-exhibitionistic self and the idealized parent imago."[46]

In the *Restoration of the Self* in 1977, Kohut delineates two configurations[47] in the concept of the bipolar self further and indicates how the mature self is developed in response to the mirroring and the idealized self-objects.[48] In his theo-

---

46) Paul Ornstein, "Introduction: The Evolution of Heinz Kohut's Psychoanalytic Psychology of the Self," Heinz Kohut, *The Search for the Self*, Vol. 1, 66.

47) "The terms 'structure' and 'configuration' are synonymous for Kohut, and he uses them interchangeably." Siegel, 66.

48) "One configuration, the grandiose self, concerns the mirroring, early maternal selfobject, whose responses accept and affirm the child's exhibitionistic narcissism. The other configuration,

retical considerations of the bipolar self,[49] Kohut focuses on examining "the disintegration of the two basic psychological functions – healthy self-assertiveness vis-à-vis the mirroring self-object, healthy admiration for the idealized self-object."[50] According to Kohut, a cohesive, independent **self arises** under a "normal, favorable" relationship with "the matrix of mirroring and idealized self-objects."[51] However, if the mir-

---

the idealized parental imago, concerns the merger with an idealized self-object that brings a sense of perfection, safety and wholeness to the self. These two configurations are components of a supraordinate configuration that Kohut calls the 'bipolar self.'" *Ibid.*, 118.

49) Siegel summarizes Kohut's understanding of the bipolar self as follows: "The bipolar self contains two poles, a pole of ambitions and a pole of ideals. The child's healthy, expansive, exhibitionistic narcissism constitutes one pole. In norma*l development the narcissism associated with this pole evolves into what eventually is experienced as ambitions. The yearning* to merge with a stabilizing, tension-regulating, idealized self-object creates the other pole. In normal development the idealizing narcissism associated with this pole evolves into what eventually is experienced as guiding ideals." *Ibid.*, 118.

50) Kohut, *The Restoration of the Self,* 171.

51) *Ibid.*, 171.

roring self-object does not respond to the exhibitionistic, narcissistic need of the child, empathically, the healthy exhibitionistic self is not developed, but instead, "an isolated sexualized exhibitionistic preoccupations concerning single symbols of greatness (the urinary stream, feces, phallus) will take over."[52] Thus, the grandiose-exhibitionistic self grows only by the empathic mirroring of the selfobject.

Likewise, if the idealized omnipotent selfobject fails to respond to the merging needs of the child, "the child's healthy and happy wide-eyed admiration will cease, the broad psychological configuration will break up, and isolated sexualized voyeuristic preoccupations with isolated symbols of the adult's power (the penis, the breast) will take over."[53] In other words, another pole of the idealized parent imago of the child grows when the idealized person empathically responds to the merging needs of the child toward the admirable selfobject, by including the child as part of the self,

---

52) *Ibid.*,172.

53) *Ibid.*

thus, making the child borrow the person's omnipotence to manage its narcissistic tension.

If the selfobject does not respond to the narcissistic needs of the child until experiencing a trauma, or, inappropriate phase, "The clinical manifestation of an exhibitionistic or voyeuristic perversion may arise."[54] Kohut explains more about clinical manifestation from the experiences of the repetitive trauma of the child as follows:

> That the perversion, the sexualized replica of the original healthy configuration, still contains fragments of the grandiose self (exhibitionism of parts of one's own body) and of the idealized object (voyeuristic interest in parts of the body of others) is to be understood as a vestige of one aspect of the original self-object constellation: ... The deepest analysis of either one of these two clinical manifestations does not, however, lead to a bedrock of drives, but to narcissistic injury and depression."[55]

---

54) *Ibid.*
55) *Ibid.*, 173.

In his explanations of the bipolar self, Kohut suggests his ideas of the nuclear self. As Kohut wants to explain the grandiose pole and the idealized pole of the **self using** the term, the bipolar self, he emphasized a core self among the many selves of a person, using the nuclear self. In other words, Kohut speaks of the grandiose self and the idealized parent imago as they represent the two poles that are located in the nuclear self among many possible selves in the person.

The nuclear self is developed during the normal process of narcissistic experiences in the interaction with selfobject. As the primary narcissism of the child that had experienced its selfobject as part of the self that was disturbed because of the inevitable limitations of the empathic responses of selfobject as well as the unwanted occurrences of unfavorable environments during an earlier stage of psychic development, "a process takes place in which some archaic mental contents that had been experienced as belonging to the self become obliterated or are assigned to the area of the nonself while others are retained within the self or are added

to it. As a result of this process a core self —the nuclear self—
is established."[56]

In fact, Kohut argued that there may be several selves existing at the same time. However, he believed that one self
is located at the center of a person's psyche which is the most
stable one[57] and that is the nuclear self. In his paper, "On
Courage," that was written in the early 1970s but published
in 1985, Kohut argues, "The nuclear self is thus that unconscious, preconscious and conscious sector in id, ego, and superego which contains not only the individual's most enduring values and ideals but also his most deeply anchored
goals, purposes and ambitions."[58]

Kohut continues explaining the importance and functional meaning of the nuclear self as follows:

This structure is the basis for our sense of being an independent

---

56) *Ibid.*, 177.

57) Mollon, 36.

58) Kohut, "On Courage," 1985, cited from Mollon, 36.

center of initiative and perception, integrated with our most central ambitions and ideals and with our experience that our body and mind form a unit in space and a continuum in time. This cohesive and enduring psychic configuration, in connection with a correlated set of talents and skills that it attracts to itself or that develops in response to the demands of the ambitions and ideals of the nuclear self, forms the central sector of the personality.[59]

According to Kohut, the sense of coherence comes from both the content of the nuclear self and the relationship with the selfobject. He argues that the psychic contents of the nuclear self are developed by the consolidation of "the bulk of nuclear grandiosity" into "nuclear ambitions" which is acquired most likely by the mirroring of "the maternal self-object" in the earlier stage, followed by that of the bulk of nuclear idealization at a later stage of childhood.[60] Furthermore, the earlier mental contents in the nuclear self are

---

59) Kohut, *The Restoration of the Self,* 177-178.
60) *Ibid.* 179.

"usually predominantly derived from the relation with the maternal self-object (the mother's mirroring acceptance confirms nuclear grandiosity; her holding and carrying al-lows merger-experiences with the self-object's idealized omnipotence), whereas the constituents acquired later may relate to parental figures of either sex."[61] Therefore, Kohut argues, "the the sense of the continuity of the self, that is, the sense of our being the same person throughout life" comes not only from the mental contents of the nuclear self but also from the relationship in which the nuclear **self interacts** with the selfobject.[62]

Kohut suggests other hypothetical factors that regulate the bipolar self or two poles of the nuclear self. He proposes a "tension gradient" that represents the relationship be-tween the two poles, and a "tension arc" that describes the overflowing psychological activity between them. He de-

---

61) *Ibid.* For Kohut's cited reference, see Kohut, "Forms and Transformation of **Narcissism**" in 1966.
62) *Ibid.*, 179-180.

scribes the ideas as follows:

> I have tried to express this hypothesis by the employment of an evocative terminology. Just as there is a gradient of tension between two differently charged (+ , -) electrical poles that are spatially separated, inviting the formation of an electrical arc in which the electricity may be said to flow from the higher to the lower level, so also with the self. The term "tension gradient" thus refers to the relationship in which the constituents of the _self stand_ to each other, a relationship that is specific for the individual self even in the absence of any specific activity between the two poles of the self; it indicates the presence of an action-promoting condition that arises "between" a person's ambitions and his ideals (cf. Kohut, 1966, 254-255). With the term "tension arc," however, I am referring to the abiding flow of actual psychological activity that establishes itself between the two poles of the self, i.e., a person's basic pursuits toward which he is "driven" by his ambitions and "led" by his ideals (ibid., 250).[63]

---

63) *Ibid.*, 180.

Therefore, in order to describe his hypothesis of the bipolar self and its functions, Kohut uses several factors such as two poles of the "grandiose self" and the "idealized parent imago," and "tension gradient" that stand to each other in the form of a "tension arc." He believed that the areas linked by the tension arc consist of basic talents and skills.[64]

According to this hypothesis, two poles regulate each other flowing through the tension arc. Thus, if one pole represents a lack of development, the other pole that is developed may compensate more in terms of the underdeveloped pole by overflowing psychological activity through the tension arc as if it charges the other pole electrically. His hypothesis implies that, for example, a person who has an underdeveloped grandiose self may compensate for his psychological structure of the self, if the idealized parent imago is sufficiently developed. In other

---

64) Otto F. Kernberg, M.D., *Aggressivity, Narcissism, and Self-Destructiveness in the Psychotherapeutic Relationship* (New Haven, CT: Yale University Press, 2004), 53.

words, although a person may show exhibitionistic narcissism due to the lack of the development of the grandiose self, there is a possibility of restoring a healthy self, if another pole of the idealized parent imago is sufficiently developed enough to compensate for the other pole through a tension arc.

Kohut believed that a person has two chances to develop the cohesive self that gives a sense of oneness and wholeness throughout life. One chance comes from the consolidated development of the grandiose self through the mirroring response from the grandiose selfobject, while the other chance is made possible when the idealized parent imago is structured firmly by the merging response of the idealized selfobject. Kohut states, "This group of processes makes its specific contributions to the formation of an ultimately cohesive self by compensating for a disturbance in the development of one of the constituents of the self via the especially strong development of the other."[65]

---

65) Kohut, *The Restoration of the Self,* 185.

He summarizes his hypothesis of developing the cohesive self in different terms as follows:

> Briefly, we can say that if the mother had failed to establish a firmly cohesive nuclear self in the child, the father may yet succeed in doing so; if the exhibitionistic component of the nuclear self (the child's self-esteem insofar as it related to his ambitions) cannot become consolidated, then its voyeuristic component (the child's self-esteem insofar as it is related to the child's ideals) may yet give it enduring form and structure.[66]

From his perspectives, it is through these two chances that one can build up his/her cohesive self. Kohut believed that pathological disorders are resulted "only from the failure of both of these developmental opportunities."[67]

According to Kohut, the child does not need a perfect selfobject in order to develop the cohesive self. Rather, pa-

---

66) *Ibid.*, 185-186.
67) *Ibid.*, 185.

rents who have limitations, due to the reality of life, are capable of nurturing the child' psychological development, if they respond to the narcissistic needs of the child empathically consistently sufficient.[68] At some point, the child would experience "the optimal frustration" that may understand and accept the limitation and reality of the selfobject. Then, the child would internalize the qualities that s/he experiences from the grandiose selfobject and the idealized selfobject into an inner psychological structure that will regulate the cohesive self through the process of "transmuting internalization."

> What a child needs is neither continuous, perfect empathic responses from the side of the self-object nor unrealistic admiration. What creates the matrix for the development of a healthy self in the child is the self-object's capacity to respond with proper mirroring at least some of the time; what is pathogenic is not the occasional failure of the self-object, but his or her chronic incapacity to

---

68) *Ibid.*, 187-188.

respond appropriately, which, in turn, is due to his or her own psychopathology in the realm of the self. As I have repeatedly pointed out, it is the optimal frustration of the child's narcissistic needs that, via transmuting internalization, leads to the consolidation of the self and provides the storehouse of self-confidence and basic self-esteem that sustains a person throughout life.[69]

As continued in his footnotes in the *Restoration of the Self* as noted below, Kohut also believed that the psychological development of an adult is incomplete, in general. He argued that the healthy adult continuously needs the selfobject. Thus, it is a natural course of life for an adult to attempt to search for the selfobject and to replace it with another when necessary.

The psychologically healthy adult continues to need the mirroring of the self by self-objects (to be exact; by the self-object aspects of his love objects), and he continues to need targets *for his*

---

69) Footnote 8 in Kohut, *The Restoration of the Self*, 187–188.

*idealization. No implication of im*maturity or psychopathology must, therefore, be derived from the fact that another person is used as a self-object — self-object relations occur on all developmental levels and in psychological health as well as in psychological illness. That the difference between health and disease is here seen to be relative, is exemplified by our reaction to depressed people: The depressed person's inability to respond to us — our incapacity to infect him with even a minimum of joy in response to our presence and to our efforts in his behalf — inevitably creates a lowering of self-esteem in ourselves, and, feeling narcissistically injured, we react to it with depression and/or rage."[70]

3. Conclusion

As I discussed thus far, Kohut's psychology of the self has distinctive contributions in understanding narcissism and the

---

70) Footnote 8 in Kohut, *The Restoration of the Self,* 188.

psychological structure of the self. Through his clinical experiences, Kohut constructed a new psychological theory of the self and created "a friendlier atmosphere in his consulting-room"[71] which was often a conflicting and confrontational space between the analyst and the analysand when the Freudian theories applied. Furthermore, Kohut suggested the transformation of the narcissism through the interaction with the analyst and the analysand that was initiated by the analyst's empathic mirroring of the narcissistic needs as well as allowance of the idealizing needs of the analysand, In other words, Kohut argued the possibility of the transformation of the narcissistic person by mirroring and idealizing empathic responses from the analyst. The possibility of the analysis and transformation of narcissistic phenomena among individual, group, and institutions as well as both positivity and possibility within Kohut's self psychology may supply creative and constructive tools for the transformation of narcissistic phenomena in our contemporary age.

---

71) Siegel, 170.

Bibliography

Ellis, Havelock. "Auto-erotism: A psychological study." *Alienist and Neurologist.* Vol. 19 (1898).

Freud, Sigmund. "On Narcissism: An Introduction." ed. Andrew P. Morrison. *Essential Papers on Narcissism.* New York: New York University Press, 1986.

Hummel, Leonard M.. "Heinz Kohut and Empathy: A Perspective from a Theology of the Cross." *Word & World,* Volume XXI, No. 1 (2001).

Kernberg, M. D., Otto F.. *Aggressivity, Narcissism, and Self- Destructiveness in the Psychoterapeutic Relationship.* New Haven, CT: Yale University Press, 2004.

Kohut, Heinz. "Remarks About the Formation of the Self." In *The Search for the Self: Selected Writings of Heinz Kohut: 1950-1978.* Vol. 2. ed. Paul H. Ornstein. New York: International Universities Press, 1978.

_____. *The Analysis of the Self; a Systematic Approach to the Psychoanalytic Treatment of Narcissistic Personality Disorders.* The Psychoanalytic Study of the Child Monograph. New York,: International Universities Press, 1971.

_____. *The Restoration of the Self.* New York: International Universities Press, 1977.

Miller, Ivan J.. "Interpersonal Vulnerability and Narcissism: A Conceptual Continuum for Understanding and Treating Narcissistic Psychopathology." *Psychotherapy: Theory, Research, Practice, Training,* Vol. 29, Issue 2 (1992).

Mollon, Phillip. *Releasing the Self: The Healing Legacy of Heinz Kohut.* London: Whurr, 2001.

Ornstein, Paul. "Introduction: The Evolution of Heinz Kohut's Psychoanalytic Psychology of the Self." Heinz Kohut, In *The Search for the Self,* Vol. 1. ed. Paul H. Ornstein. New York: International Universities Press, 1978.

Pulver, Sydney E.. "Narcissism: The Term and the Concept." ed. Andrew P. Morrison, M. D., *Essential Papers on Narcissism.* New York: New York University Press, 1986.

Siegel, Allen M. *Heinz Kohut and the Psychology of the Self.* New York, NY: Routledge, 1996.

Strozier, Charles B.. *Heinz Kohut: The Making of Psychoanalyst.* New York: Other Press, 2001.